SOUL
PURITY

A WORKBOOK FOR COUNSELORS AND SMALL GROUPS

David A. Coats

First Edition: 2016

Soul Purity is a revised edition of *Building a Pure Life*, originally
published in 2012

Printed in the United States of America

ISBN: 978–0–9899532–2–1

Published by www.greatwriting.org

Typesetting: quintapress.com

Cover design: www.greatwriting.org

Dave Coats's *Soul Purity* is a rich, robust, relational resource. Other materials on this vital topic often move toward extremes: they are either too abstract or they are so "practical" that they lack a theological foundation. This work, on the other hand, beautifully balances theological depth with practical implementation. Coats's focus on the heart and conscience reminds me of the great Puritan soul physicians who blended the holiness of God and the horrors of sin with the forgiveness of Christ and the wonders of grace. I highly recommend this Christ-focused, gospel-centered workbook.

Bob Kellemen, Ph.D., Chair of the Biblical Counseling and Discipleship Department, Crossroads Bible College

Our small group used this resource for several weeks in an intense discipleship study. The most remarkable thing is the flexibility in design. It can be used in private or group study and should be used in both.

Bill Hallady, Staff writer, Brainerd Baptist Church, Chattanooga TN

In a world filled with trash
disguised as cheap pleasure,
some have exchanged the wonder
and the glory of God
for the weak repulsiveness of man

Contents

Foreword

*S*oul Purity has been forged in the battlefield of personal sanctification as pastor and biblical counselor, Dave Coats, has fought for purity in this muddy world. Also, having worked with people in this area of spiritual struggle for many years, he concludes that the best way to help people who already lack personal discipline and self-control is to provide a workbook format that "forces" them to study the Word of God daily. Over an eight-week period of manageable daily lessons, Dave systematically dismantles the heart idols that surround the sins of impurity, and gradually builds a new and powerful sense of the greatness and goodness of God. The mind is nurtured with daily readings, songs, meditations, and questions, all intended to renew the heart in the process.

Structured Approach

If someone is incredibly self-motivated and determined to break with their sensual sins, then they will find this a good structured resource to work through on their own. However, most people who are losing the battle with lust will likely need someone in their lives—a biblical counselor, pastor, or friend—to help push them through the workbook. If you are losing more than winning, and you really want to win, take this book to someone you can trust and ask them to keep you accountable with the daily readings and exercises.

Pre-emptive strike

This is also a good workbook for "prevention," a sort of pre-emptive strike, especially for teenagers. Maybe parents could ask their teenage children to work through it to weaken sin before it gets its roots in too deep, and also to build up defensive walls through raising the twin bulwarks of the goodness and greatness of God.

Four Features

I especially appreciate four features in this book.

- First, the *God-centered focus.* There's no question that delighting in God is the most powerful enemy of sin. Dave's relentless focus on the greatness and goodness of God will produce deep humility before God as well as profound love for God.
- Second, throughout and especially in the appendix, *it deals honestly, bravely, and plainly with masturbation.* No punches pulled. Straight between the eyes. Repent of this sin.
- Third, it does what very few other books on this subject do. *It calls into serious question the reality of conversion if people keep falling into this sin.* Through personal testimonies, Dave shows that one of the greatest ways we can love people is not to say, "Oh, well, God forgives, it's tough, no one's perfect, etc."

Rather it's to say, "How can you do this and say you know and love God?" If in the past the church has been too unforgiving of those who fell into sexual sin, we are certainly at risk today of "over-forgiving" in the sense that we rarely question the compatibility of repeated offending with real conversion.

• Fourth, the weekly focus on the cross, keeps hope alive and points all sinners and saints to the only source of purity for the head, the heart, and the hand.

Dr. David Murray,
http://headhearthand.org,
Professor at Puritan Reformed Seminary
and Pastor of Grand Rapids Free Reformed Church,
and author of *Jesus on Every Page*, *Christians Get Depressed Too*,
and *How Sermons Work*

Preface

Mission Statement

The purpose of discipleship in life purity is to practice necessary *patterns of protection from evil* (standards we set up personally), to develop the *pursuit of a holy God* (allowing His *goodness and greatness* to move us), and to build *open and honest relationships* so that believers will love God supremely and hate evil continuously.

This work is the result of a number of studies I have carried out to help people build a life of purity. The goal is to help them turn from what seems to be satisfying and pleasurable but is found to be sinful and destructive to the total fulfillment found in Christ. I hope that through this, readers will begin to rebuild their view of God.

I worked on this book while spending a week with my family on the East Coast, close to the beach. The need to address the issues discussed in this study was reinforced by the seemingly continual exposure to temptation and worldly attractions we experienced there. Men and women of God cannot be hermits and retreat from the world God has called them to reach, yet some families and individuals are choosing such isolation, having as little to do with the outside, unsaved world as possible. However, what they often find in the process is that they take the desire for the things of the world into their homes. Why? Because the problem isn't the world: it is the sinful desires of our hearts.

The opposite response is not good either. Assimilating into the world—becoming like it by accepting its philosophy, standards, values, and pleasures—turns Christians into people who are irrelevant. They become no different from those they are called to reach with the gospel that changes lives. Godly believers need to go out into their cultures and neighborhoods with hearts that are engrossed with the glory of God. We must refocus on God so that we can show Him to our world.

Pastors, deacons, women who teach Sunday school, wives who are alone, and the multitudes of Christians coming out of our churches looking for something other than an irrelevant Christianity are crashing and burning on the runways of life. We must address the problem of purity destruction that is happening today. As Christian students arrive at college each fall, a high percentage of them are already struggling with purity. The Word of God has the answers to this problem. We need to get into it and find God's help to be pure people in a world overcome by sensuality in all its forms.

I thank all those who have had a part in helping me with this study and giving me suggestions as to what needs to be addressed or included. It has been my privilege to counsel and disciple many men and women over the last couple of decades of ministry. Being a youth pastor, camp director, and now a pastor has helped me interact with many people who have come looking for help. Being in a college setting for the last decade has increasingly challenged me with the need to put together materials that will help disciple those who are trapped in their own worlds of lust. Furthermore, raising three teens into adults has given me a fresh burden to help young people love God with their whole hearts and be less attracted to the world that wants to capture their souls. I hope this study is a right step in that direction.

I would like to dedicate this work to two people. The first is my dad, who labored quietly in obscurity, planting churches in North America. God has given Dad much fruit for his labor.

The second is my wife, Judi, who has patiently encouraged me and prayed for me through my own journey from lust for cheap things to a longing for our glorious God. Judi, you have made this journey an incredible one (often full of laughter), always mirroring the love of God for a sinner in your love for me. Thank you for editing and checking my writing.

Dave Coats
Longview Farm, Pembine, Wisconsin

My Testimony

Each of us has a journey to take. This journey is what the Bible calls "the Christian life," or "becoming like Christ." This journey is only possible for those who know Christ. I began my journey at the age of seven. By that time I had already been exposed to cheap pornography magazines which I found in a field and which were passed around by older guys in the neighborhood. As a teenager my lust was fueled through TV, books, and destructive relationships with girlfriends. Christian college helped me learn that I should say "no," but that was all I knew. "Memorize verses and avoid temptation," I was told. "God hates this sin." I understood that. But as I tried to change my thought-life and sensual desires, a huge battle was taking place in my inner man. Getting married did not help. Studying theology in seminary did not win the battle for me. Heading to the mission field did not solve my struggle. As a youth pastor I prayed with young men and helped them look at Scripture to see how wrong pornography in the mind is. We memorized verses such as "flee youthful passions" (2 Tim. 2:22). But for me, something seemed to be missing. Why? Eventually I would feel that the battle was too strong again and I was going to fall.

So when the Internet was created I was stunned. I saw the Internet as a huge hole of sensual depravity into which men (including myself) would fall. Up to that point the issues were "Be willing to turn off the TV, say 'no' to friends who want to watch porn videos, and turn away from magazines and books in the store." Now we really had a problem. How to escape? How could we be pure? "The apostle Paul certainly did not deal with Internet pornography," I thought to myself. But in my desperation to help others and help my own feeble, spiritual life become strong and biblically pure, I looked in the Bible for the hope and help I had not before considered. I knew that I could not simply hibernate to hide from the attacks of Satan. If Paul could minister the gospel with thousands of ritual prostitutes in town and all forms of fornication going on outside in the streets, surely he had answers.

When I began working with college men and realized for the first time how widespread this problem was (not just Internet pornography as such but specifically the battle with the lusts of the flesh) I decided I needed to pursue intensely the biblical means to gain personal and corporate help in battling the idolatry of the heart. Several books and studies got me going in the right direction. I appreciate those who have gone before me in this field. Interestingly, women have now joined men in this struggle against the sensually saturated mind. Our culture is inundating us with sensual images and our minds are becoming saturated with sensuality, irrespective of gender.

I am especially burdened that this process of turning from the cesspool of sensuality to the awesome glory and beauty of Christ begin in the local churches and our homes. I believe that waiting till college years is too late. God gave us the home and the church in which to build believers, and we must do so in those places. As I recently met with the elders and small-group leaders of an inner-city church, I encouraged them to "get the conversation going" among the men about their struggles with the sensuality of our culture. They have to get past the superficial discussions of life to the deeply spiritual and personal part of who we are. You will notice that I have put notes to small-group leaders throughout this study.

I am confident that what God has done to change my heart into a place where He is cherished, worshiped, and seen as supreme can happen in your heart too. I pray that you will commit yourself to this process so that your journey will be one of grace and truth, wrapped in the cross of Christ.

How To Use This Book

In a study such as this the danger is that, despite all my good intentions to be of help to you, there will still be something lacking in the presentation of the material that keeps you from gaining the desired benefit. So I hope that this brief overview will help you get started well and follow the direction of the workbook.

Workbook Layout

The material has been laid out so that you can work through it day by day over eight consecutive weeks (or longer if you slow down and take extra time on parts of it). This process of meditation is the most practical and helpful way to benefit, as most struggles go in cycles and most temptation points arise in similar situations. By following the daily schedule you will be helped daily to think through scriptural principles and to meditate on God's nature. In order to gain the maximum benefit it is vital that you commit to working through the book for the whole of the eight weeks, if not longer, rather than dipping in from time to time.

There is a daily meditation focus every day except Day 7. The Scripture passages selected focus on aspects of the goodness and greatness of God and reflect ways of expressing His glory, majesty, power, and works. Sometimes the focus is on creation and the Creator; other times it is on God's sustaining grace toward us or a great event in which God has shown the world His power. Take time to allow these events or words to make God real to you. I cannot emphasize too much how necessary this daily God focus is for you. You may understand all the truth and be able to answer all the questions, but if you do not fill your heart daily with God you will miss replacing the cheap, earthly pleasure of sensuality with the glorious wonder of Almighty God.

The need for this activity can be illustrated by imagining that someone has become infected with a virus after stepping on a nail. This person can take aspirin, drink lots of water, take vitamins, and do all the other good things that people do to maintain or even build the body. But the infection is gaining steadily, moving through the body. Antibiotics are needed to directly attack it. Nothing else will work. Likewise, meditation on the wonder and pleasure of knowing the God of glory is the only thing that is sufficient to make a sensual thought-life and sexual struggles appear cheap and wicked and thus no longer so appealing. Reminding ourselves of the cross and God's goodness magnifies in our hearts the riches of His glorious work toward us and humbles us so that we want to find our total fulfillment and joy in Him alone.

Note to small-group leaders: Please check how the people in your group are doing in their meditation on God. If they are struggling with this activity, take them to "Before We Go Further" just before the start of Week 3 and work through the material there. Help them to see the difference between knowing information and memorizing truth, and really having a heart that embraces their position in Christ and the glory and goodness of God.

The end of each week (Day 7) is structured to help you reflect on the cross and God's goodness. This focus is particularly well suited for a Sunday. Doing this at least once a week is critical, but you may decide that the focus on the cross is something you want to include daily. Each week on Day 7 we will take a journey through the events of the last twenty-four hours of Christ's life before his crucifixion. We need to take time to expose our hearts fully to the reality of this event. The journey into the Garden of Gethsemane and on to Golgotha should be a regular walk in our mind's eye that we take to experience afresh the effects of our sin and the commitment of our Savior to redeem our wretched, vile lives from the depths of hell.

Part of the meditation material is worship through music. Very few things in life encourage us in our pursuit of purity like music can and will if used correctly. Thus, it is essential that our music draw us to God. Our music should be true to Scripture. It should celebrate God's character and glory. The Psalms give examples of how people praised and exalted their God in song. God inspired the psalmists to write words that reflected a deep passion for His glory and holiness. Don't be satisfied with shallow music. Never accept a cheap version of God in music. Don't compare a glorious and eternal God to low and worldly things. God is beyond compare and above all things on this earth. Your music should never bring God down to man's level (in Rom. 1:19–23 God explains how this happens). Instead, our music should bring us up to God.

In order to build your meditation on God and renew your mind in Him, choose songs and hymns that lift up God, His grace, His mercy, His love, and His sacrifice on the cross.[1] Find hymns that help you marvel at the holiness and majesty of God. Then use these songs and hymns on a daily basis. I have found that the best way to begin my day is in praise to God through one of these great and wonderful explosions of worship. I am so grateful for those who can write words that express how great God is. If you visit my house in the morning you will most likely find me on my treadmill, enjoying God through these songs. I don't care what the rest of my household thinks of my musicality at that point: I am enjoying the wonder of a great God. I have included some examples of hymns and songs to encourage you in the joy of worship and praise.

Note to small-group leaders: *Get the members of your group to share with one another how God has used the Scripture passages, the music, and the focus on God to penetrate their hearts and change their longings and joys during the week. When they start sharing about God it is a powerful encouragement to others in the group. They need to see that godly men and women can and should share their struggles and the spiritual joys of their hearts. You, the leader, should be the first one to get the conversation going on temptation and also joy in God. Let them know that you aren't perfect, but that you are pursuing God. Openness may come slowly in your group. Encourage it. Model it.*

The sidebar material, questions, and other helps are an integral part of this book. On this page is an example of what one of these sidebars will look like when you fill it in. Make the most of these opportunities to reflect on what you are reading and studying.

The Goal

The goal of this workbook is to see Ephesians 4:22–24 and Colossians 3:9–19 worked out in our lives. Memorize one of these two passages and meditate on its meaning for you as a believer. You must give yourself to this task of becoming Christlike (Rom. 8:29).

For Counselors, Disciplers, Mentors, and Local-Church Small-Group Leaders

ASSESSING THE INVOLVEMENT

You will need to distinguish the level of involvement in pornographic material and sensual struggles in the lives of those you are discipling. Some people may only recently have been exposed to these temptations. They may not have been interested in them before or they may have been sheltered from them. They

> Write out your thoughts on the wonder of the cross.
> *When I think on the cross, it does not take long for me to come face-to-face with my sins. Sometimes I stop and consider some of the specific sins that put Christ on the cross. When I take time to thank God for Gethsemane and the cross, my heart is moved.*
>
> Take time to read, sing, and meditate on the words of the song "My Redeemer" and write out how this is a blessing to you.
> *This song always challenges me to appreciate God and my redemption. He paid the price. I know that, but until I stop and consider this price, I am not deeply affected by this truth. I am so thankful that He could pay the price for my sin.*

require what I call "Level 1 involvement." The intensity of their struggle and the degree of temptation they face will be less for them than for others. Don't make assumptions based on their age. Interview them and question them about how long it has been going on, the frequency of the struggle, and the extent of defeat suffered. Find out what help has been received up to this point and who knows about this struggle other than you.

Others need more specific help in becoming pure in life. They require "Level 2 involvement." They have struggled on and off for some time and probably have developed some level of masturbation activity. They have established patterns of choosing wrong desires and seeking to satisfy them. Their heart-desires have been turned toward thoughts and actions that they hate to admit. They do not find satisfaction in their sin and are trying on their own to solve this before it "gets too big or costs too much." Alternatively, they may have made a few halfhearted attempts to get help from those who don't know how to solve the problem other than by "saying no."

"Level 3 involvement" concerns a depth of sin and degradation that has no end in sight. People at this level are burdened by their hidden lives, the depths of wickedness to which they have fallen, and the amount of chaos this addiction has caused, and they feel that there is little that can be done. They have no hope of ever leaving this trash behind. They have lived it out, acted it out, and found themselves doing things they vowed they would never do. These people need others to help them take intense and drastic measures so that they can set themselves apart to seek God. *Note that, if this has been their lifestyle for a while, you may want to go to Week 8 early in the process to check out the reality of their spiritual lives.* There is a huge difference between a person who struggles with pornography and one who has lived with it for a good period of time and now sees it as a "normal" part of life. For the latter, you have to figure out why this person has reached this point. If he or she just did not understand how victory was possible, that is a very different problem from knowing but not changing.

Note to small-group leaders: *Think about how these different levels of struggle will affect interaction in the local-church setting. Things you should look for are (1) group members who don't speak out at all; (2) group members who talk of purity as something they have dealt with and from which they have now moved on; (3) others who say that this was never a problem for them; (4) those who are satisfied with occasional forays into sensuality and masturbation, but who don't see the need to change. Remember, those who are not entrenched in pornography don't feel too bad. They know people who are far worse off than them. Those who are entrenched in failure as a life pattern won't speak out because they fear being labeled as an "addict" rather than someone Christ is rescuing from sin. They may feel that an "addict" will be ostracized. We have to find ways to gain the confidence of those in our groups. Use the one-on-one times outside the group sessions to assure members individually of your love and God's love for them.*

Furthermore, we know that victory in the struggle to put away pornography or say "no" to the temptation is not the main goal. This only deals with the surface issue. Recently, I sat in a session with a well-known counselor/author who related how, early in his dealings with addicts, he focused on this surface level of sin, only to miss the underlying cause. The man he counseled gave up his addiction to drugs, only to replace it with an addiction to long-distance running. The man left his family, got involved in ultra-marathon competitions, and is now a major success in this area.

You are seeking to find out what drives this lust for sensual pleasure in those you are helping. Finding the source of their sensuality will not be something that you can accomplish in one discipleship or counseling session. Over time you will need to work out what drives and motivates them in life. What do they want most? What do they feel they have been missing in life? What one thing will make the difference for them?[2] This pinpointing of their heart-idols will show you what *really* needs to change. It is the one god that must be dethroned in their hearts. The heart of the matter is, what is the matter with the heart?

Notes

1 Through counseling people I have found that the theology of the cross is critical to the heart that would be pure. Beginning each day of our journey close to the foot of the cross helps us avoid the problem of Rom. 2:1–5 while pursuing the good of verse 4. We should daily be drawn by God's goodness and mercy to a humble walk with Him. Focusing on the cross will do this.

2 See **David Powlison's** list of "X-ray questions" to expose the "Idols of the Heart" in Appendix 6.

Week 1.
Reset the Conscience

Remember that these meditation themes are the key to renewing your heart. You must give yourself time with God every morning. You must find your satisfaction in Him. I recommend you commit to spending somewhere between ten and thirty minutes daily in this communion with God. Your problem is not first and foremost the pornographic images in your brain; it is your idolatrous heart seeking comfort, satisfaction, and pleasure in something other than your God. It is this idolatrous heart that seeks its solace in pornographic and sensual images.

Day 1. What Is the Conscience ?

Daily Meditation Themes

- *Goodness of God:* "I will give thanks to the LORD with my whole heart" (Ps. 9:1); "and the grace of our Lord overflowed for me with the faith and love that are in Christ Jesus" (1 Tim. 1:14).
- *Greatness of God:* "In the beginning, God created the heavens and the earth" (Gen. 1:1).

Song: "How Great Thou Art"

O Lord my God, when I in awesome wonder
Consider all the works Thy hand hath made,
I see the stars, I hear the mighty thunder,
Thy pow'r throughout the universe displayed:

Then sings my soul, my Saviour God, to Thee,
How great Thou art, how great Thou art!
Then sings my soul, my Saviour God, to Thee,
How great Thou art, how great Thou art!

But when I think that God, His Son not sparing,
Sent Him to die, I scarce can take it in:
That on the cross, my burden gladly bearing,
He bled and died to take away my sin.

When Christ shall come with shout of acclamation
And take me home, what joy shall fill my heart!
Then I shall bow in humble adoration,
And there proclaim: My God, how great Thou art![1]

Meditation

It is helpful to spend some time looking at a biblical explanation of the conscience so that we can pave the way for victory in our battle for purity. As believers we know that we have the Holy Spirit within us (Rom. 8:9). This presence of the Spirit is the fulfillment of a great promise given by God to his children. We will never

What did you enjoy about God today?

_____

_____

_____

_____

_____

_____

_____

_____

_____

_____

_____

_____

_____

_____

_____

_____

_____

_____

_____

_____

_____

_____

_____

_____

_____

_____

_____

_____

_____

_____

23

Take time to thank God for His moral compass that He implanted within you. Ask Him to help you keep it true to His Word and sensitive to His Spirit.

_____
_____
_____
_____
_____
_____
_____
_____
_____
_____
_____
_____
_____

Assess how you have drifted in your setting of your conscience.

_____
_____
_____
_____
_____
_____
_____
_____
_____
_____
_____
_____
_____
_____
_____
_____
_____
_____
_____
_____
_____

lose the Spirit. He is the down payment for our eternal salvation. He is also our teacher, guide, comforter, and helper in time of prayer—to list just a few of his activities. We can quench the Spirit, the apostle Paul tells us (1 Thes. 5:19); we can also grieve the Spirit; but he will always continue to do his work within our hearts. Not all people have the Spirit, but all people do have a knowledge of God and of what is right.[2]

The conscience is not the same as the Spirit of God. The conscience is like the alarm of our souls. All people have a conscience at birth and will battle their conscience up to a certain point. This God-given characteristic of humans makes us unique; in this respect we are different from the animal creation around us. We are implanted with the knowledge of good and evil. The problem is that we come into this world dead in sin and determined to turn from God. This bent away from God is the basis for our rebellion against Him and our desire for autonomy. Our consciences remind us that this is a problem. However, we can work against our consciences and what we innately know to be right.

When we receive salvation, we acquire a new sense of what is undesirable and unacceptable. However, this sense of right and wrong can be adjusted. The world slowly influences us to accept what was initially despised. The self starts to desire that which our new natures in Christ show us to be undesirable and unacceptable. We adjust what our consciences respond to and so begin to ignore God's truth and His criteria of right and wrong. Some of this is even done under the guise of "grace." How perverted![3]

When through the Scriptures we realize that we have drifted from our once pure walk and passion for God, we desire that simplicity and purity again. We want to have our consciences alert us to those times when temptation appears and to those places we need to avoid. Conscience is not our guide, but it is a guard that we can set near our hearts.

Notes

1 Tr. from the Russian by **Stuart K. Hine** (1899–1989).

2 Rom. 1:18–20 explains man's natural state.

3 Read Jude's explanation of the twisting of grace in Jude 4.

Day 2. How We Set the Conscience

What do you see about God here?

_____
_____
_____
_____
_____
_____
_____
_____
_____
_____
_____
_____
_____
_____
_____
_____
_____

What does it mean to be complete in Christ alone? Make this thought personal and praiseworthy.

_____
_____
_____
_____
_____
_____
_____
_____
_____
_____
_____
_____
_____

Daily Meditation Themes

- *Goodness of God:* "I will be glad and exult in you; I will sing praise to your name, O Most High" (Ps. 9:2). "How precious is your steadfast love, O God!" (Ps. 36:7).
- *Greatness of God:* "Who has measured the waters in the hollow of his hand, and marked off the heavens with a span, enclosed the dust of the earth in a measure and weighed the mountains in scales and the hills in a balance? … Whom did he consult, and who made him understand? Who taught him the path of justice, and taught him knowledge, and showed him the way of understanding? Behold, the nations are like a drop from a bucket, and are counted as the dust on the scales; behold, he takes up the coastlands like fine dust" (Isa. 40:12–15).

Song: "Complete in Thee"

Complete in Thee! no work of mine
May take, dear Lord, the place of Thine;
Thy blood hath pardon bought for me,
And I am now complete in Thee.

Yea, justified! O blessed thought!
And sanctified! Salvation wrought!
Thy blood hath pardon bought for me,
And glorified, I too, shall be!

Complete in Thee! no more shall sin,
Thy grace hath conquered, reign within;
Thy voice shall bid the tempter flee,
And I shall stand complete in Thee.

Complete in Thee—each want supplied,
And no good thing to me denied;
Since Thou my portion, Lord, wilt be,
I ask no more, complete in Thee.

Dear Saviour! when before Thy bar
All tribes and tongues assembled are,
Among Thy chosen will I be,
At Thy right hand, complete in Thee.[1]

Meditation

In order to be truly broken over our sin (expressing godly sorrow and repentance), we must see our thoughts and actions the way God does. Understanding the biblical concept of the heart is crucial to helping reset the conscience.

We must understand how the Bible describes the innermost part of man. In a biblical sense, "the heart" is made up of three parts: mental, emotional, and volitional. It is immaterial, but in some ways it is more real than any other part of man. The heart is part of what makes humankind different from the rest of creation. We are rational beings (i.e., able to think and choose for ourselves) who make moral choices based on good and evil. We are influenced by our old nature, which desires to live for self; but as children of God we have a new nature that moves us to desire right ways before God. Jesus said that what we are and what we do come directly from the heart (Matt. 12:34; 15:18–20). According to how we think in our hearts—how we purpose in our inner being and desire in our hearts—so we will be.

In today's Christian culture and popular literature very little is written about the heart. Focusing on outward actions and symptoms, however, does not help people. You can change a person's habits (don't go to that porn store), you can stop the influences (don't watch that porn flick), you can have a person do good things (memorize Scripture and pray every day), but if you have not addressed the longings, desires, passions, and beliefs that drive this person to wicked and lewd behavior, you will not see a long-term change in his or her life. The writer of Proverbs 4:23 instructs us

Dave's testimony: I have found that one of the best ways for me to keep a sensitive conscience is to have others help me check to see if my standards are helping me. I must, however, avoid making my standards my badge of holiness. Instead, my standards should be a tool to keep me steadfast in my purity and godliness.

I remember my pastor quoting these words: "Sow a thought and reap an act; sow an act and reap a habit; sow a habit and reap a character; sow a character and reap a destiny."

Catalogue the many areas of influence in your life. Now start writing out which kinds of input are dangerous for you personally. Why?

_____
_____
_____
_____
_____
_____
_____
_____
_____
_____
_____
_____
_____
_____
_____
_____
_____
_____
_____
_____
_____
_____
_____
_____
_____
_____
_____
_____

Note: Be ready to discuss with your small group the specifics of your struggle.

to keep a strong guard around our hearts. On the other hand, Jesus commanded us to love God with all our inner being—our hearts. How do we go from keeping evil out of our hearts to having a love for God fill our hearts?

Understand that the heart is separate from the brain. Sometimes we hear people describe our difficulties in life as resulting from problems with our understanding (brains); they do not mention the involvement of our hearts. This is not accurate biblically and theologically. What makes this so bad is that if we don't have an accurate view of the problem, we won't have a proper plan for change. We might even excuse pornography because we are told we are not able to control our brain function.

The best way to describe our inner being is by thinking of our brains as the physiological processors of information (see diagram). All the "input" we send to the brain is received. The brain does not make the choice to hear or not hear sensual stories. *The brain does not lust.* The brain does not desire to watch pornography. The brain simply captures every image we send it. What happens immediately is that our hearts are affected. One day we will become "brain dead": the physical organ called the brain will stop functioning. However, at our core or in our hearts we will still function. We will have a conscious existence forever.

In fact, it is our hearts that decide whether to accept or reject those images and imprints we send to the brain. The heart desires more semi-pornographic viewing to satisfy its immoral appetites.[2]

The heart lusts. The brain does not. Immediate interaction takes place between my mind (the thinking part of my heart) and my emotions (the feeling part of my heart) as the images and events play out before me.

My passions, longings, and desires are

The heart and conscience

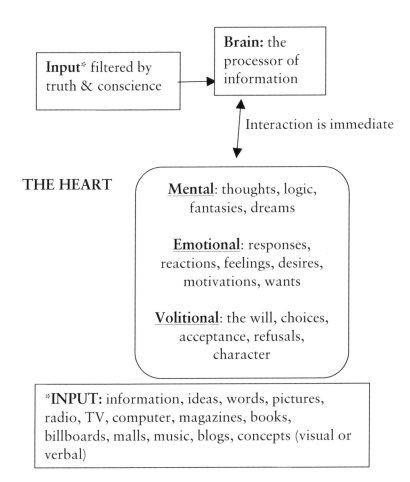

cranked up so that I can enjoy the sensual input my heart has decided to take in. I have decided to take in that sensuality.

The will (the other part of my heart) is already influenced by the way I have thought through this event and how I have been affected in my desires by it. My will is now overwhelmed by the amount of feedback it has received that is of a sensual, worldly, and fleshly nature. My conscience is just along for the ride, as will, desires, and thinking have reset their sensitivity to accept the sensual input.

Now I will choose to go down this path to the cesspool of sensuality again and again, feeling as if I can't change. I will say, "I'm addicted to something that controls

Journal some thoughts about the lusts, passions, and desires of your heart.

_____
_____
_____
_____
_____
_____
_____
_____
_____
_____
_____
_____
_____
_____
_____
_____

Small groups: Help one another sort out the biblical difference between "heart" and "brain."

_____
_____
_____
_____
_____
_____
_____
_____
_____
_____
_____
_____
_____
_____
_____
_____

me." But what really controls me? My heart. My passions. My desires. Those are the parts of my inner being that I have fed again and again.

Notes

1 Aaron R. Wolfe (1821–1902).

2 "The heart, according to scripture, not only includes the motives, feelings, affections, and desires, but also the will, the aims, the principles, the thoughts, and the intellect of man. In fact, it embraces the whole inner man." **Robert B. Girdlestone,** _Synonyms of the Old Testament_ (Grand Rapids, MI: Eerdmans, 1973), 65.

Day 3. Passages That Help Picture Sin

Daily Meditation Themes

- *Goodness of God:* "The LORD lives, and blessed be my rock, and exalted be the God of my salvation" (Ps. 18:46). "My people are bent on turning away from me, and though they call out to the Most High, he shall not raise them up at all … My heart recoils within me; my compassion grows warm and tender. I will not execute my burning anger; I will not again destroy Ephraim; for I am God and not a man" (Hosea 11:7–9).
- *Greatness of God:* "Behold, God is exalted in his power; who is a teacher like him? Who has prescribed for him his way, or who can say, 'You have done wrong'? Remember to extol his work, of which men have sung. All mankind has looked on it; man beholds it from afar. Behold, God is great, and we know him not; the number of his years is unsearchable. For he draws up the drops of water; they distill his mist in rain, which the skies pour down and drop on mankind abundantly. Can anyone understand the spreading of the clouds, the thunderings of his pavilion? Behold, he scatters his lightning about him and covers the roots of the sea. For by these he judges peoples; he gives food in abundance. He covers his hands with the lightning and commands it to strike the mark. Its crashing declares his presence" (Job 36:22–33).

Song: "'Tis Not That I Did Choose Thee"

'Tis not that I did choose Thee,
For Lord, that could not be;
This heart would still refuse Thee,
Hadst Thou not chosen me.

Can you sense God's sadness and holiness expressed to His people? But can you also see Him reach out to them and offer them the relationship He has chosen them for? How does this mirror His goodness to us?

31

Take time to use biblical terms to describe your own sin. Use them in prayer to God. Thank Him for His forgiveness for your corrupt heart and its wicked choices and longings.

_____
_____
_____
_____
_____
_____
_____
_____
_____
_____
_____
_____
_____
_____
_____
_____
_____
_____
_____
_____
_____
_____
_____
_____
_____

Small groups: Help one another to watch out for unbiblical labels or terms when discussing the sins of the heart.

Thou from the sin that stained me
Hast cleansed and set me free;
Of old Thou hast ordained me,
That I should live to Thee.

'Twas sovereign mercy called me
And taught my opening mind;
The world had else enthralled me,
To heavenly glories blind.
My heart owns none above Thee;
For thy rich grace I thirst;
This knowing, if I love Thee,
Thou must have loved me first.[1]

Meditation[2]

Some time ago, I spent a number of weeks counseling a college man who was overwhelmed by a struggle that he desired to quit. He came to me seeking help in the battle. It took me a while to realize that, although he did not like doing the action (masturbation), no one had ever really spent time showing him biblically why it was wrong before God. He said he had tried to stop it, but that it was difficult since no one had ever shown him why God would call this action "sin."[3] I recommended that he meditate on Bible verses that could help him visualize sin the way God sees it.

The more we view our acts, thoughts, desires, and motives as God does, the more we will make choices that reflect desires, thoughts, and passions that are driven by the glory of God. This change of heart is the first step in the process of turning from our sin back to God. We will not hate our sensual thoughts, pornographic tendencies, and illicit activities unless we realize that God calls them evil. In the Bible God often gives us pictures that help us gag over our sin. If we are revolted by our sin, we are much more likely to remove it from our lives. The passages that we will look at below are helpful in this process of renewing our minds and rejecting the filth within our hearts.

Thus a prerequisite to using these passages on sin is that we recognize that our thoughts, actions, and desires are wicked. It is very helpful to use the exact terminology for sin, and descriptions of it, that God uses in the Bible: iniquity, evil, corrupt, putrid, abomination, rebellion, filthiness, unrighteousness, lust, corruption, and wicked.

ISAIAH 1:4–6

Ah, *sinful nation, a people laden with iniquity*, offspring of *evildoers*, children who deal *corruptly*! They have forsaken the LORD, they have despised the Holy One of Israel, they are utterly estranged. Why will you still be struck down? Why will you continue to rebel? The whole head is sick, and the whole heart faint. *From the sole of the foot even to the head, there is no soundness in it, but bruises and sores and raw wounds*; they are not pressed out or bound up or softened with oil [emphasis added].

One way to help us turn from our sin is to see it as puss oozing from a sore, as with a wound that has gotten infected and is not cleansed. When you sit down at your computer to enjoy and fulfill your lusts through pornographic images, you must see yourself as sitting down to drink up some puss and infection into your soul. Paul uses a similar image in 2 Timothy 2:17, when he speaks of sin as gangrene—something that is deadly, sickly, and must be destroyed.

EZEKIEL 16:2–6

Son of man, *make known to Jerusalem her abominations*, and say, Thus says the Lord GOD to Jerusalem: Your origin and your birth are of the land of the Canaanites; your father was an Amorite and your mother a Hittite. And as for your birth, on the day you were born your cord

Journal:

was not cut, nor were you washed with water to cleanse you, nor rubbed with salt, nor wrapped in swaddling cloths. No eye pitied you, to do any of these things to you out of compassion for you, but you were cast out on the open field, for you were abhorred, on the day that you were born. And when I passed by you and saw you *wallowing in your blood*, I said to you in your blood, "Live!" I said to you in your blood, "Live!" [emphasis added].

Another image that God uses concerning sin is that of the blood and mess of birth. He pictures our sin—our abominable desires for adultery and fornication—as the mess that is cast aside after birth. It is something not desired but loathed. So it should be with our views of our thoughts and acts of sensuality. We must loathe and hate them. They must be disgusting to us. You don't see a father or mother enjoying the afterbirth when a newborn baby comes into the world. Instead, parents focus on the beauty of the cleansed and bathed newborn child.

EZEKIEL 24:3–13

And utter a parable to the *rebellious house* and say to them, Thus says the Lord God: "Set on the pot, set it on; pour in water also; put in it the pieces of meat, all the good pieces, the thigh and the shoulder; fill it with choice bones. Take the choicest one of the flock; pile the logs under it; boil it well; seethe also its bones in it. Therefore thus says the Lord God: *Woe to the bloody city, to the pot whose corrosion is in it*, and whose corrosion has not gone out of it! Take out of it piece after piece, without making any choice. For the blood she has shed is in her midst; she put it on the bare rock; she did not pour it out on the ground to cover it with dust. To rouse my wrath, to take vengeance, I have set on the bare rock the blood she has shed, that it may not be covered. Therefore thus says the Lord God: Woe to the bloody city! I also will make the pile great. Heap on the logs, kindle the fire, boil the meat well, mix in the spices, and let the bones be burned up. Then set it empty upon the coals, that it may become hot, and its copper may burn, that its uncleanness may be melted in it, its corrosion consumed. She has wearied herself with toil; its *abundant corrosion* does not go out of it. Into the fire with its corrosion! On account of your *unclean lewdness*, because I would have cleansed you and you were not cleansed from your uncleanness, you shall not be cleansed anymore till I have satisfied my fury upon you" [emphasis added].

A third image God uses is that of a pot which has a crust of leftover food stuck at the bottom. No one will want to eat any of the food put in that pot. It is not useful. It needs to be boiled and cleansed of its filth. The scum must be removed. Similarly, a pattern of pornography, immoral desires, and base pleasures will leave a scum on your soul that will take much purifying to remove.

2 PETER 2:17–22

These are waterless springs and mists driven by a storm. For them the gloom of utter darkness has been reserved. For, speaking loud boasts of folly, they *entice by sensual passions of the flesh* those who are barely escaping from those who live in error. They promise them freedom, but they themselves are *slaves of corruption*. For whatever overcomes a person, to that he is enslaved. For if, after they have escaped the *defilements of the world* through the knowledge of our Lord and Savior Jesus Christ, they are again entangled in them and overcome, the last state has become worse for them than the first. For it would have been better for them never to have known the way of righteousness than after knowing it to turn back from the holy commandment delivered to them. *What the true proverb says has happened to them: "The dog returns to its own vomit, and the sow, after washing herself, returns to wallow in the mire"* [emphasis added].

Our final word picture refers to sin in a vivid way. Peter says that our sin is like the vomit coughed up by a dog. The dog has no problem going back to that pile of vomit and eating it up again. This is like a sinner who returns again and again to his or her abominable and sensuous pleasures in order to feast the flesh on the trash of the world. Somehow, we are blinded to what this pile of vomit is really doing to us.

Notes

1 **Josiah Conder,** 1836.

2 I am indebted to **Steve Gallagher** for getting me thinking biblically in this direction (**Steve Gallagher,** *On the Altar of Sexual Idolatry* [Dry Ridge, KY: Pure Life Ministries, 2000]).

3 See Appendix 5, "The Struggle with Masturbation," for counsel on this particular subject.

Journal:

Day 4. Godly Sorrow and Repentance (1)

Journal your thoughts about the greatness of God:

_____
_____
_____
_____
_____
_____
_____
_____
_____
_____
_____
_____
_____

Can you see yourself in Psalm 113:7? Are you poor? Are you needy? In what ways?

_____
_____
_____
_____
_____
_____
_____
_____
_____
_____
_____
_____
_____
_____

Daily Meditation Themes

- *Goodness of God:* "He raises the poor from the dust and lifts the needy from the ash heap" (Ps. 113:7).
- *Greatness of God:* "The LORD is high above all nations, and his glory above the heavens! Who is like the LORD our God, who is seated on high, who looks far down on the heavens and the earth?" (Ps. 113:4–6).

Song: "Worthy of Praise"

My heart overflows with praise to the Lord
I will lift up my voice to the King
He brought me out of the pit of despair
And taught my heart to sing

Worthy of all my praise
You are worthy of all my praise
I bow at your throne, and I worship you alone
Lord, You are worthy, worthy of praise

My lips sing His praise, My heart feels His love
His Word is a lamp to my way
His mercy and grace forever endure
His arms draw me closer each day[1]

Meditation

What is the point of the passages we have studied about God's view of sin? The point is to help us come to real repentance, driven by a sorrow toward God.

As it is, I rejoice, not because you were grieved, but because you were grieved into repenting. For you felt a godly grief, so that you suffered no loss through us. For godly grief produces a repentance that leads to salvation without regret, whereas worldly grief produces death. For see what earnestness this godly grief has produced in you, but also what eagerness to clear yourselves, what indignation, what fear, what longing, what zeal, what punishment! At every point you have proved yourselves innocent in the matter.   (2 Cor. 7:9–11)

In this passage Paul explains that when someone is found or exposed in sin, that person has two options. He or she can respond either with worldly sorrow or with godly sorrow. How do we know which kind of sorrow we have experienced? Sorrow of a worldly sort is evidenced when the person is motivated by what people will think of him or her. Such sorrow is all horizontally directed. The person has not yet been broken and is not sorrowful toward God. Godly sorrow, on the other hand, is vertical: it sees God, self, and sin in their proper proportion and position. God is holy and on His throne, while I am wretchedly sinful before Him. God, in mercy and love, reaches out to turn me toward His holiness and grace. How do I respond? Do I hate being "caught" in my sin? Or am I so thankful that God cares enough to turn me 180 degrees back toward His righteousness? To be like Him, I must turn.

A man was once caught in a lie about his sensuality. He wept and cried. When I talked to him, he spoke about the shame this lie would bring upon his family and his name. He was worried about losing his ministry. As I listened to his concerns and fears I heard nothing of what God thought about this. I heard nothing of his sorrow over having offended a holy God and having dragged God's name through the mud. He was more concerned for his own reputation than God's. This man had no sorrow toward God. He had no desire to turn back to God; rather his only concern was to save his own family and name.

In the Bible, Joseph said that he could not commit adultery with Potiphar's wife because

Think about the last time God exposed your sin. How did you respond? Walk through it in your mind, looking for evidence of your view of God.

_____

_____

_____

_____

_____

_____

_____

_____

_____

_____

_____

How has God redeemed and changed you?

_____

_____

_____

_____

_____

_____

_____

_____

_____

_____

_____

_____

Small groups: Take time to discuss what these steps of repentance will look like in the local church. How will your family and church body know this change is real?

What would "earnestness" look like for you in the area of sensuality?

_____

_____

_____

_____

_____

_____

_____

_____

_____

_____

_____

_____

_____

_____

Small groups: We know that our inner man will lie to us about what "earnestness" means. So you need to be honest and open with the members in your group and ask them to keep you accountable about how careful you are. One man wrote an e-mail to members of his small group confessing that he was careless about his TV watching while his wife was away, and that this carelessness then led to carelessness in his Internet use. As he e-mailed them the same night that he fell, his honesty became a platform for forgiveness and openness.

he was concerned for God's name and his relationship with God (Gen. 39). He had a high view of God, and his focus on God kept him from immorality. He also had the right view of sin. Godly sorrow begins with seeing the enormity of your sin against a holy God. Your heart must be deeply moved by the selfishness of your life and its focus on your wicked desires.

What evidence will there be in your life of godly sorrow of the heart?

- *Change in your thinking and view of God:* Everything that we do in life flows from our actual view of God. He is holy, majestic, pure, beautiful, all-knowing, always present, all-powerful, loving, gracious, righteous, and sufficient. We may say we believe that God sees everything and that He loves us enough to expose our sin and bring us back to Himself, but do we really and truly believe it? Does our view of God drive our purity of life? Do we find our ultimate satisfaction in Him?

- *Change in your thinking and view of self:* I am weak and driven by pleasure rather than strong in God's grace and driven by love for Him.

- *Change in your thinking and view of sin:* Sin is wicked abomination against God.

In 2 Corinthians 7 Paul explained what he saw in the lives of those driven by godly sorrow. Over the next few days we will be looking at some of the words he used in verse 11 to describe their turning away from the cesspool and seeking the purity of God. Here are the first two.

EARNESTNESS

The meaning is earnest care, the opposite of indifference and neglect.

- Those who have godly sorrow show great concern over the path they take.

- They are careful about the places they visit and the things they watch.
- They do not neglect to keep their hearts focused on God.
- There is an *earnestness* about their walk. No careless attitudes are allowed.

We tend to become apathetic when we forget how vulnerable we are to Satan's attacks.

- We tend to become indifferent when we lose our sense of God's hatred for sin.
- God's Word and God's people will help us to watch out for apathy in our choices, thoughts, motives, and longings.
- Having the right view of our life stories and how they fit into the big picture of God's plan is crucial. If a soldier thinks his night-watchman duties are not that important, he will get careless. We can't afford to be careless.

TO CLEAR

The word Paul uses here comes from the Greek *apologia*, meaning a defense against attacks. "Defense" is a word we often associate with apologetics (defense of the faith). What about a defense of our purity?

How will we defend ourselves against the attacks of Satan?

- How will we conduct our lives so we are without blame?
- How will we choose our daily patterns of life so that Satan has no foothold?
- Can we clear ourselves before God? How does God view us today?
- Is our life an apologetic for His glory. The more we live in ways that demonstrate the right view of our God, the more we defend His character accurately.

Note

1 **Ron Hamilton.** © 1996 by Majesty Music, Inc. All rights reserved. Used by permission.

Day 5. Godly Sorrow and Repentance (2)

_____
_____
_____
_____
_____
_____
_____
_____
_____
_____
_____
_____
_____

When you feel as if God is so great that He is too big to know you or care about you, what should you do?

Small groups: Talk about those times in your group and see how you can encourage one another in this battle for a pure heart. We must battle the lies about God perpetuated by self and Satan.

_____
_____
_____
_____
_____
_____
_____
_____
_____

Daily Meditation Themes

- *Goodness of God:* "I will bless the Lord at all times" (Ps. 34:1). "[He] saved us and called us to a holy calling, not because of our works but because of his own purpose and grace, which he gave us in Christ Jesus before the ages began" (2 Tim. 1:9).
- *Greatness of God:* "Where were you when I laid the foundation of the earth? ... Who determined its measurements—surely you know! ... Or who shut in the sea with doors when it burst out from the womb, when I made clouds its garment and thick darkness its swaddling band ...? ... Have you commanded the morning since your days began, and caused the dawn to know its place ...? Have you ... walked in the recesses of the deep? ... Can you bind the chains of the Pleiades or loose the cords of Orion? ... Do you know the ordinances of the heavens? Can you establish their rule on the earth? Can you lift up your voice to the clouds, that a flood of waters may cover you?" (Job 38:4–5, 8–9, 12, 16, 31, 33–34)

Song: "Be Thou My Vision"

Be Thou my Vision, O Lord of my heart;
Naught be all else to me, save that Thou art.
Thou my best Thought, by day or by night,
Waking or sleeping, Thy presence my light.

Be Thou my Wisdom, and Thou my true Word;
I ever with Thee, and Thou with me, Lord;
Thou my great Father, I Thy true son;
Thou in me dwelling, and I with Thee one.

Riches I heed not, nor man's empty praise,
Thou mine Inheritance, now and always:

Thou and Thou only, first in my heart,
High King of Heaven, my Treasure Thou art.

High King of heaven, my victory won,
May I reach Heaven's joys, O bright Heaven's Sun!
Heart of my own heart, whatever befall,
Still be my Vision, O Ruler of all.[1]

Meditation

Continuing our study of 2 Corinthians 7:11 we see that the four words we will study next carry with them a level of emotion and passion. This is good. Their combined weight should cause us to realize that there is a need for heart emotions and desire that will drive us toward God and away from sensuality. We will cover two today and two tomorrow.

I should never live the Christian life as a stoic. Stoic Christianity is not biblical living. I am to live passionately for God and be driven by His glory. Paul said in Philippians 3:10 that he lived life for one purpose and it drove him. He was not halfhearted—ever. The stuff of life that goes against God and denies Him His glory should incite my inner being with a strong desire to live for His holiness and glory. I can get excited about living for God!

INDIGNATION

The word means inner pain, anger, vexation. I should carry within me a certain amount of inner pain over my falling into sin: grief that I could be foolish enough to fall into sensual sin, grief that Satan trapped me, and grief that I gave my own flesh such an opportunity to overcome God's grace. If God has forgiven me, I need not carry a weight of shame toward him.

FEAR

This means terror, fright. Good fear drove Joseph to flee from fornication (Gen. 39). He feared sinning against God. We should fear

---

What things are you passionate about? How do they compare with God? How can you gain a passion for God-ward living?

_____

_____

_____

_____

_____

_____

_____

_____

Small groups: How can you encourage one another in this passion for God?

_____

_____

_____

_____

_____

_____

_____

_____

Ask God for an inner fear of sin and a hatred of its effects.

_____

_____

_____

_____

_____

_____

_____

_____

God, not man. But I also must fear what sin will do to me. This fear is not that God will thrash me, but that I will lose the opportunity to give Him glory and will instead bring shame to His name.

Note

1 Attributed to **Dallan Forgaill;** tr. from ancient Irish to English by **Mary E. Byrne,** 1905, and versed by **Eleanor H. Hull,** 1912.

Day 6. God's Goodness and Greatness

Daily Meditation Themes

- *Goodness of God*: "Oh, magnify the LORD with me, and let us exalt his name together! ... Oh, taste and see that the LORD is good!" (Ps. 34:3, 8). "But thanks be to God, who gives us the victory through our Lord Jesus Christ" (1 Cor. 15:57).
- *Greatness of God*: "Can you find out the deep things of God? Can you find out the limit of the Almighty? It is higher than heaven—what can you do?" (Job 11:7).

Song: "Holy, Holy, Holy"

Holy, holy, holy! Lord God Almighty!
Early in the morning our song shall rise to Thee;
Holy, holy, holy! Merciful and mighty!
God in three Persons, blessed Trinity.

Holy, holy, holy! All the saints adore Thee,
Casting down their golden crowns around
    the glassy sea;
Cherubim and seraphim falling down before Thee,
Who was, and is, and evermore shall be.

Holy, holy, holy! Though the darkness hide Thee,
Though the eye of sinful man Thy glory may not see;
Only Thou art holy; there is none beside Thee,
Perfect in pow'r, in love, and purity.

Holy, holy, holy! Lord God Almighty!
All Thy works shall praise Thy name, in earth,
    and sky, and sea;
Holy, holy, holy; merciful and mighty!
God in three Persons, blessed Trinity![1]

Meditation

We continue looking at words from 2 Corinthians 7:11.

Journal your thoughts about God:

_____

_____

_____

_____

_____

_____

_____

_____

_____

_____

What did Christ do that should help us see victory? How can that victory be real?

_____

_____

_____

_____

_____

_____

Small groups: When someone fails, do you tend to condemn or encourage? Do you judge or help that person get back on track? Why?

_____

_____

_____

_____

_____

_____

_____

_____

43

Ask God for a new desire for His glory. Write out how such a desire will change your daily pattern of life.

_____
_____
_____
_____
_____
_____
_____

Small groups: Share these ideas with at least one other person in your group.

_____
_____
_____
_____
_____
_____

What will you do for the kingdom of God before you die? Will your life matter in eternity? It should if you live with eternal values.

_____
_____
_____
_____
_____
_____
_____

LONGING

This word expresses vehement or earnest desire. You must have a longing for God that will outweigh any desire your flesh may have for sin. You must a longing that resembles that of a thirsty deer for water (Ps. 42:1). What was formerly a longing for lustful pleasure and cheap thrills for your flesh must be replaced by a holy affection in your heart for a holy God. We must want to be satisfied with Him.

ZEAL

Zeal is a powerful emotion that moves us to be or do something. Within your heart there must be a new drive to live for God. The typical zealot of New Testament times was driven by the cause of Jewish patriotism. He would give his life for this cause. He would sacrifice himself and die to see the nation out from under the heel of Rome. Within the heart of the believer comes a similar zeal—but for holiness and God's pleasure. Believers will sacrifice all else for the cause of God's holy kingdom.

Another zeal in our hearts should be that of sharing the power of the cross and the hope of the resurrection with a world that is powerless and hopeless. If we don't see how much we have to share with those around us, and what a difference it will make to them, it is not surprising that we don't have zeal.

Our final word may catch us by surprise. We may not expect to see this word in a passage explaining life after repentance. However, we must look at the big picture. What is going on here is a battle for the heart and life of mankind.

PUNISHMENT

This word speaks of revenge or justice. We should desire to take back all the life we can from the hands of the destroyer. Satan will do whatever he can to destroy the name and cause of Christ, but he can only do this through the evil hearts and deeds of men and women. So our desire must now be to get back at him for every day he had us in bondage. We must live our lives daily for God in such a way that we do damage to Satan's kingdom and build God's.

I cannot begin to tell you about those who wish they could take back choices they made or days they lived. Interestingly, I have never had people tell me they regretted staying pure. I have never had those I counseled saying they wished they could have had more of the world instead of enjoying the glory of God.

One final thought on finding pleasure in God: He designed us to know the satisfaction of His presence. Psalm 36:7–9 is a great passage that considers God, His character, and what He does for His people. The psalmist speaks of the joy of knowing God's lovingkindness, and then says that those who make their refuge "in the shadow" of God's wings "feast on the abundance of [God's] house." Those who would drink of God find "the river of [God's] delights." That is our God.

Note

1 **Reginald Heber,** 1826.

Thank God for saving you from the cesspool. Now consider the treasure you have in Christ. Write out what God has reserved for you in heaven.

Small groups: Discuss Romans 8:18–30 and Paul's explanation of "groaning" and "glory" that includes our inheritance.

Do you long for God's kingdom? Spend time in prayer, asking God for a heart that longs to be with Him rather than wrapped up in this world.

Day 7. Focus on the Cross

Write out your thoughts about what you are reading. This is vital if you are to let the full sense of the cross event sink into your heart. If you find it helpful, write out a prayer of thanks to God which mentions the details of what the Son of God did on the cross.

Small groups: Explain what this event in the Garden shows about the manhood of Christ. Talk about the strength of character and body demanded in order to deal with all that Christ faced here and on the cross.

Each week we should set aside a particular time to focus on the cross. Romans 2:1–4 tells us that we need to be reminded often of the "riches" of God's goodness and patience. This activity will bring us to regular points of repentance and restoration in a pure walk with God.

This morning we will think through the time Christ spent in the Garden in agony for us and will walk with Him from Gethsemane to the high priest's house.

Turn to Matthew 26:36–46 and allow this text to have full impact on your mind and emotions. Can you sense what Christ is experiencing in the Garden? Can you grasp the battle that is taking place within His body—a battle so intense that the Gospel writers use terminology connected with a physical heart attack to describe it ("My soul is very sorrowful, even to death," Matt. 26:38)? Continue reading verses 57–68 so that your heart can fully take in the scene and the emotions as these ungodly men attack Christ and treat him so rudely. Consider what he faced there for you. Feel the blows and the spit. Think about Christ's humiliation and His meekness (ultimate power under control) on your behalf to sink in. He took this for you. The hatred, anger, and bitterness of the priests can be felt as they treat Him so shamefully. He did this in your place, and in mine. We should have felt these insults and blows. Our bodies should have been bruised and beaten. Instead, it was the divine Son of God who took it all for us.

You have to picture men whose hearts were so filled with anger and jealousy that only their pharisaical law kept them from finishing the job they wanted to do on Christ. They would have killed him, but their consciences were limited by their view of the law. This hatred flowed out into a small mob scene where they took the opportunity to beat him up. They should have been thankful that the Son of God did not let loose the "hosts" of heaven to defend Himself, nor did He speak a word, which would have consumed them in an instant.

Daily Meditation Theme
- *Greatness of God: " … That they may know that you alone, whose name is the* LORD, *are the Most High over all the earth"* (Ps. 83:18).

Song: "The Old Rugged Cross"

On a hill far away stood an old rugged cross,
The emblem of suffering and shame;
And I love that old cross where the dearest and best
For a world of lost sinners was slain.

So I'll cherish the old rugged cross,
Till my trophies at last I lay down;
I will cling to the old rugged cross,
And exchange it some day for a crown.

O that old rugged cross, so despised by the world,
Has a wondrous attraction for me;
For the dear Lamb of God left His glory above
To bear it to dark Calvary.

In that old rugged cross, stained with blood
    so divine,
A wondrous beauty I see,
For 'twas on that old cross Jesus suffered and died,
To pardon and sanctify me.

To the old rugged cross, I will ever be true,
Its shame and reproach gladly bear;
Then He'll call me some day to my home far away,
Where His glory forever I'll share.[1]

Why is this song so powerful? What does the writer express for us that should consume our hearts?

_____
_____
_____
_____
_____
_____
_____
_____
_____
_____
_____
_____
_____
_____

Small groups: In what ways do shame and reproach help us conform to Christ? (Consider Rom. 8:28–29.)

_____
_____
_____
_____
_____
_____
_____
_____
_____
_____
_____
_____
_____
_____

The pain of these events is intense. From the garden to the cross, Jesus feels the impact of sin. Jesus can't bypass these events. He must deal with them on our behalf. Satan will throw everything he can at Christ, hoping Jesus will turn back and quit. But that won't happen. It did not happen. Jesus deals with the confrontation of evil by His finishing the path before Him, feeling every blow, every word, and most of all, every ounce of sin laid on Him by the Father.

Note

1 **George Bennard,** 1913.

Week 2.
Win the Battle

We have now seen that setting the conscience correctly is the first step in winning the battle for purity of heart. Without true repentance we will not see long-term change. Understanding how the heart works and how the conscience is affected should encourage you to press forward in this fight for a pure, inner man that can worship God.

Next, we want to look at several key passages of Scripture that help us understand what is going on in our spiritual walk in this world. They picture for us the battlefield, explain the plan for victory, and point the way to great hope when failure seems so normal.

Day 1. Understand Your Position in Christ (1)

Daily Meditation Themes

- *Goodness of God:* "Delight yourself in the LORD" (Ps. 37:4). "As a deer pants for flowing streams, so pants my soul for you, O God. My soul thirsts for God, for the living God" (Ps. 42:1–2). "Blessed be the God and Father of our Lord Jesus Christ, the Father of mercies and God of all comfort" (2 Cor. 1:3).
- *Greatness of God:* "He stretches out the north over the void and hangs the earth on nothing. He binds up the waters in his thick clouds … He has inscribed a circle on the face of the waters at the boundary between light and darkness. The pillars of heaven tremble and are astounded at his rebuke. By his power he stilled the sea" (Job 26:7–8, 10–12).

Song: "I Run to Christ"

I run to Christ when chased by fear
And find a refuge sure.
"Believe in me," His voice I hear;
His words and wounds secure.
I run to Christ when torn by grief
And find abundant peace.
"I too had tears," He gently speaks;
Thus joy and sorrow meet.

I run to Christ when worn by life
And find my soul refreshed.
"Come unto Me," He calls through strife;
Fatigue gives way to rest.
I run to Christ when vexed by hell
And find a mighty arm.
"The Devil flees," the Scriptures tell;
He roars, but cannot harm.

I run to Christ when stalked by sin
And find a sure escape.
"Deliver me," I cry to Him;
Temptation yields to grace.
I run to Christ when plagued by shame
And find my one defense.
"I bore God's wrath," He pleads my case—
My Advocate and Friend.[1]

Meditation

For a few days we will be looking at Romans 6–8. These three chapters contain the essential truth that must be the basis of your walk with God. If you expect to grow in holiness, you must understand what Paul says here. Although it is not possible for us to exposit each verse, we will take a concise enough look at each section so that those who desire to see their way clear to victory can gain hope in what God has already done.

Christ has given us victory over the flesh (6:1–14). There are three important verbs in this section: "know," "consider," and "present." The word "know" (e.g., v. 2) reminds us that there is specific truth about what Christ has done for us that it is crucial to remember daily. He has conquered sin's death-hold on man. As you listen to Paul's explanation in these first few verses, your heart should be greatly encouraged. There is nothing more for you to do in Christ that will win the war over sin. He has done all the work of salvation. He has conquered the power of sin once and for all. You could never do that. So why do you not know this? Does it not seem real? Do you struggle with the daily reality of what Paul is saying? Are there times when you really feel as if sin still controls you? If you do not accept that Christ has put sin to death and that there is nothing more you can do, you will be in for a long battle. You will be struggling in your flesh to do what Christ alone can do as the God-Man. Your human efforts will always fall short and you will live as if sin still has a mighty stranglehold on your heart and life. This is tragic. You must know what He has done for you.

Paul's words in verse 4 tell us that the goal of our being united in Christ through identification with Him in baptism is that we should walk in newness of life. This baptism is

Meditation thoughts on God: personalize what you are reading. Make this God your God.

What are your struggles with faith? Why is faith critical to a pure life?

_____

_____

_____

_____

_____

_____

_____

_____

_____

_____

_____

_____

_____

_____

Small groups: As a group, assess whether your hearts believe and desire to live this truth. Why or why not?

_____

_____

_____

_____

_____

_____

_____

_____

_____

_____

_____

_____

_____

the placing of every believer into the Body of Christ at regeneration. Not all believers have been immersed in water, but all believers have been placed "into Christ" (v. 3) at salvation. Because of this event we have the promise that the "body of sin" (our sin nature) has been "crucified," which means that we should no longer serve sin (v. 6). So, although there may be discussion about what has been destroyed, it is evident that the result is good. We do not have to serve sin. This was not true of us before our salvation; then, we had no choice but to live by our sinful drives and motives. Pornography and other life-dominating habits were unconquerable unless a selfish motive was offered. But now we have the ultimate motivation of living up to our righteous standing before God. He sees us as perfect, justified in Christ. So walk "in him" says Paul (Col. 2:6).

The word "consider" (v. 11) helps us practice the walk of faith. We have to believe that what Paul says about sin is true. We could say, "Make it true" or "Live it out." The Greek word is sometimes translated "reckon," and this accounting term points to the need to move the truth of Christ's victory over sin from the theological realm to the practical realm of our daily lives. Theology must always impact our daily lives, otherwise it is simply knowledge about something, not knowledge for something. Theology should affect how we act and think, yet we don't always match our theology on paper with our theology in practice. I can tell what you really believe about God by the decisions you make and the actions you do. I choose to believe that God says my sin does not have to dominate me anymore. Likewise, you must act as if sin does not have to rule you anymore. Paul says, "Don't let sin reign or rule you anymore" (see v. 12). You do not have to obey your lusts and drives. Instead, you can obey your desires for God and His kingdom righteousness. Notice that Paul is appealing to his readers' new desires, to the new person within. Don't give in to lust and cheap pleasures. You don't need to do that. You have the opportunity to serve righteousness (v. 13).

The word "present" (v. 13) helps us take the steps of action based on what is true. We submit ourselves to righteousness rather than to the lusts of the flesh. When under our old masters, sin and self, we had no choice; we submitted to their every whim and desire. We were dominated by our fleshly, worldly, ungodly hearts that wanted whatever we thought was best. What I wanted ruled my heart. What God wanted did not matter. What parents and others said did not matter, unless it interfered with my happiness. I was controlled by my master called "Self," and Self was extremely arrogant, proud, and consumed with getting pleasure *now*.

My new master is Christ. My new goal is righteousness and holiness. I am no longer under the "law" of sin (v. 14). This law was a terrible master, but now I am under the master called "Grace" that liberates me to live for Christ, not self. So Paul says that those who say that life under grace removes any standards or fences have totally missed the point of salvation (v. 15). We have been saved from sin, not saved so that we can sin. We are either worshipers of God and servants of righteousness, or worshipers of self and servants of sin (vv. 16–17). The latter statement is definitely true of the lusting idolater who worships his or her sensual pleasures, choosing to submit to their longings and to serve the flesh, and who constantly goes back into the life that was so deadly.

- The flesh is the old nature I am born with

Why do you think it is so difficult to submit to God? What happened in the Garden of Eden (Gen. 3) that forever changed our relationship with God in this life?

_____

_____

_____

_____

_____

_____

_____

_____

_____

Small groups: How do the words "autonomy" and "rebellion" help us understand this battle?

_____

_____

_____

_____

_____

_____

_____

_____

_____

_____

_____

_____

_____

How were you a "prisoner" before you were saved? Do you still feel like one now—a prisoner to lust and filth?

_____

Small groups: Discuss which thoughts, desires, and longings tend to open the door for the "old master" of sin and the flesh. What kinds of tyrants do you find them to be?

_____

and which dominates me before I am indwelt by the Spirit.

- Christ's death conquered sin's hold over me.
- Christ's resurrection guaranteed victory. God looks at me through the blood of Christ. I am justified.
- The sin nature (the old man, the flesh) no longer has control or dominion over me. I must live like it!
- I must choose to believe this to be true. I can and must choose to live for God in the Spirit every day (Rom. 6:15–23).
- When I submit to sin's reign, I do so willingly. Sin does not automatically rule me.

Note

Day 2. Understand Your Position in Christ (2)

Daily Meditation Themes

- *Goodness of God:* "Be exalted, O God, above the heavens! Let your glory be over all the earth!" (Ps. 57:5). "But I will sing of [God's] strength; I will sing aloud of your steadfast love" (Ps. 59:16).
- *Greatness of God:* "So man is humbled, and each one is brought low … Enter into the rock and hide in the dust from before the terror of the LORD, and from the splendor of his majesty. The haughty looks of man shall be brought low, and the lofty pride of men shall be humbled, and the LORD alone will be exalted in that day" (Isa. 2:9–11).

Song: "Oh for a Thousand Tongues to Sing"

Oh for a thousand tongues to sing,
My great Redeemer's praise,
The glories of my God and King,
The triumphs of His grace!

My gracious Master and my God,
Assist me to proclaim,
To spread through all the earth abroad,
The honors of Thy name.

Jesus! the name that charms our fears,
That bids our sorrows cease;
'Tis music to the sinner's ears,
'Tis life, and health, and peace.

He breaks the pow'r of canceled sin,
He sets the prisoner free;
His blood can make the foulest clean,
His blood availed for me.[1]

Meditation themes about God:

55

What assurance can you find in the last section of Romans 8?

_____

_____

_____

_____

_____

_____

_____

_____

_____

_____

_____

_____

_____

_____

Small groups: How can you use Romans 8:28–34 when Satan tempts you to quit? Discuss this question in your group.

_____

_____

_____

_____

_____

_____

_____

_____

_____

_____

_____

_____

Meditation

Continuing our study in Romans 6–8 we see that the struggle we face in the flesh is not new to believers, since even the apostle Paul wrestled with his flesh (7:4–25). It is a good sign if you have a battle going on within; it is evidence of a relationship with God that is real. No battle? No new life. Think about the dynamic truth we learned yesterday, that we no longer have to serve sin as the rest of this world does. Hallelujah!

We can even be thankful for the law, since it is the very tool that God gave to show us our sinfulness and our need for Christ (vv. 7–12). But Paul does not stay in sin's grip. He says he is thankful to God through Christ for the victory in serving God ("the law of God" is a concept pleasurable to Paul in 7:25).

Realize, then, that you are not the only one who is wrestling with impure thoughts and a pornographic world. Satan knows that this is a spiritual battle in which good people fall. Many fine pastors and godly laypeople will struggle and not come out as victors. Why? Because this is a lifelong struggle that must be taken seriously, albeit with confidence that we can and should win. At a session for men given at Northland International University in 1992, Dr. Douglas McLachlan told his audience to "plan to win."[2]

God has given us His Spirit to help us in our struggles. This is good news for the lonely believer (8:1–17). We must daily choose to walk under the Spirit's control. If you do not have the Spirit of God within you, you are not a child of God (v. 9). For those who are children of God, the promise is that we do not fight this battle alone. We must take advantage of His presence within our lives. This Spirit brings life (v. 10). The plan for this life is to "put to death" the deeds of the body so that we can live for the things of God (v. 13). This mortifying of the deeds of the body is the exact work which must take place on the basis of Romans 6 theology. Putting to death old desires which lead to sensual acts must take place in the life and heart of a spiritually alive person.

Notes

1 **Charles Wesley,** 1739.

2 Session entitled "Conquering Impure Thoughts", December 8, 1992.

Day 3. Understand the Battle

Meditation themes on God:

_____
_____
_____
_____
_____
_____
_____
_____
_____
_____
_____
_____
_____

Allow the thought of being in God's presence and worshiping Him to fill your heart today. If you worship Him, how will this help in the battle for a pure heart?

_____
_____
_____
_____
_____
_____
_____
_____
_____
_____
_____
_____
_____

Daily Meditation Themes

- *Goodness of God:* "[God] only is my rock and my salvation … Trust in him at all times … pour out your heart before him" (Ps. 62:6, 8). "[He] has also put his seal on us and given us his Spirit in our hearts as a guarantee" (2 Cor. 1:22).
- *Greatness of God:* "Give thanks to the LORD, call upon his name, make known his deeds among the peoples, proclaim that his name is exalted. Sing praise to the LORD, for he has done gloriously; let this be made known in all the earth. Shout, and sing for joy … for great in your midst is the Holy One of Israel" (Isa. 12:4–6).

Song: "All Hail the Power"

All hail the power of Jesus' Name!
Let angels prostrate fall;
Bring forth the royal diadem
And crown Him Lord of all.

Ye chosen seed of Israel's race,
Ye ransomed from the fall,
Hail Him who saves you by His grace
And crown Him Lord of all.

Let ev'ry kindred, ev'ry tribe
On this terrestrial ball
To Him all majesty ascribe
And crown Him Lord of all.

O that with yonder sacred throng
We at His feet may fall;
We'll join the everlasting song
And crown Him Lord of all.[1]

Meditation

First, look at Romans 8:28–39. This section

reminds us of Romans 6 and the reality of our position in Christ. He has done all this for us so that we can live for Him. Paul tells us that nothing can separate us from the love of Christ. We must believe that we do not "perform" spiritual works in order to make God like us or love us. Nor does our falling into sin—even the most sensual and immoral acts—cause Him to stop loving us (vv. 31–37). Some of us need this reminder. We feel that we have failed God again and again. We gave in to immoral activities or surrendered to selfish sexual pleasure. How can God love us? We may feel like dirt before Him. But Christ died for us and made us His own; we are His chosen people and part of His beloved family (vv. 31–32). If He could give His Son for us when we were not even His people, how much more will He care for us now we are His children? Nothing can cause God's love to lessen toward us. No failure before man or accusation by demonic powers will separate us from God in Christ Jesus (vv. 38–39). Hallelujah! What a Savior!

Now look at Galatians 5:16–26. This passage highlights for us the distinct battleground of our lives and hearts. We either walk in the Spirit or we walk in the flesh. The flesh and the Spirit continue to war against each other throughout our lives. They do not live happily together. When Paul speaks of the "flesh" he is not speaking of our body parts. Our bodies are not evil. Our struggle is not with our arms or our legs; it is not even with our brains (as we saw in our first week's study). The problem is with our hearts. And whether or not we feed our stomachs or provide certain comforts for our bodies, our "flesh" will be as strong and as wretched as ever. The flesh wants its desires fulfilled so that every self-focus and earthly passion can be satisfied. Yet we have the Spirit within us to help us desire to please and walk with God. *Our satisfaction through the Spirit*

Apply Romans 8:29–34 to yourself: what is your identity in Christ?

Small groups: What is the battle? Where does it take place? Be honest and specific with the other members of your group.

Think of some practical ways to deny the flesh.

_____

_____

_____

_____

_____

_____

_____

_____

_____

_____

_____

_____

_____

_____

_____

Small groups: Which old ways of your life don't seem so "corrupt" until you look at Christ and His holy character? Help one another see this sinfulness.

_____

_____

_____

_____

_____

_____

_____

_____

_____

_____

_____

_____

_____

_____

is found in Christ alone. As long as we keep feeding the flesh and giving in to its drives, we will not walk in a manner pleasing to God. We could go and live in a cave just as monks did in the past. They thought that they would flee the world and its wickedness by living as hermits. But they found that within the walls of their cave dwelt a monster. This monster, called the flesh, was full of cravings for something beyond food, drink, clothes, and shelter.

Denying the flesh, with its strong desires, is the first step in following Christ and is part of the fruit of the Spirit. You must die to self, fleshly drives, and worldly patterns every day. You can choose to enjoy God's Spirit and His fullness as you submit to His every leading. But you cannot live for God and follow Christ while enjoying pleasing self. You will choose one or the other. The most blessed thing is to arrive at the point where what you most take pleasure in is God. Christians today need to understand this, especially as many react against a form of Christianity that has rules, regulations, or standards. Instead, they embrace another kind of Christianity that accepts many of the activities mentioned in Galatians 5:19–21. Apparently, we are not to judge those who do such things, because they "love God." The result is that the "walk" for these believers looks very much like a life that is lived in the flesh and not in the Spirit. In verse 24 Paul nails such deeds as those things that should be crucified— especially the affections and lusts that drive them. This is exactly what you are called to do. Crucify or put to death these passions.

Paul says something similar in Ephesians 4:17–32, when he uses two opposing verbs, "put off" and "put on" (vv. 22, 24). Notice that the old way of living was "corrupt through deceitful desires," while the new self is "created … in true righteousness and holiness." In between those two commands is the exhortation to renew the mind (v. 23). A new heart, with new thoughts and new desires, is the focal point of this battle. You will be living in one direction (the old self) or the other (the new self). Too often, I believe, we emphasize the putting off, or denying, self, but we neglect the putting on of godliness. We get tired of saying "no" to self and fleshly lusts, but we have not learned the exercise toward godliness that daily drives us to the Rock of our salvation.

Christ did not tell His disciples merely to deny self. They were to take up their cross and to follow Him (Luke 9:23). The concept Jesus expresses in this teaching is to forget about the self entirely; to lose sight of personal interests and desires and to *follow*—a verb used of a soldier who follows a captain, or a student who follows a master or teacher.

Note
1 **Edward Perronet,** 1779–1780.

Day 4. Understand the Problem of Strongholds

Meditation themes on God:

_____

_____

_____

_____

_____

_____

_____

_____

_____

_____

_____

_____

_____

_____

_____

_____

What is it like to find your safety in God?

_____

_____

_____

_____

_____

_____

_____

_____

_____

_____

_____

_____

_____

_____

_____

_____

Daily Meditation Themes

- *Goodness of God:* "The righteous shall be glad; they shall exult before God; they shall be jubilant with joy!" (Ps. 68:3). "But thanks be to God, who in Christ always leads us in triumphal procession, and through us spreads the fragrance of the knowledge of him everywhere" (2 Cor. 2:14).
- *Greatness of God:* "Oh that you would rend the heavens and come down, that the mountains might quake at your presence … to make your name known to your adversaries, and that the nations might tremble at your presence! When you did awesome things that we did not look for, you came down, the mountains quaked at your presence" (Isa. 64:1–3).

Song: "He Hideth My Soul"

A wonderful Savior is Jesus my Lord,
A wonderful Savior to me;
He hideth my soul in the cleft of the rock,
Where rivers of pleasure I see.

> *He hideth my soul in the cleft of the rock,*
> *That shadows a dry, thirsty land;*
> *He hideth my soul in the depths of His love,*
> *And covers me there with His hand.*
> *And covers me there with His hand.*

A wonderful Savior is Jesus my Lord,
He taketh my burden away;
He holdeth me up, and I shall not be moved,
He giveth me strength as my day.

When clothed in His brightness, transported I rise,
To meet Him in clouds of the sky,
His perfect salvation, His wonderful love,
I'll shout with the millions on high.[1]

Meditation

Let's look at 2 Corinthians 10:4–5. The term "strongholds" used in verse 4 refers to something like a castle or fortress. We know that in Bible times it was normal for a kingdom to have castles or fortresses that guarded the king and acted as a defense for his kingdom. When invaders came to attack, they had to overcome the protective measures taken to defend the city and its inhabitants. Along with the city walls, the castle or fortress was built to protect that which was most valuable. Within were those who were loyal to the king. Also somewhere within the walls, in an area well-guarded by the king's soldiers, were his treasure and his family.

Paul draws us a quick picture to illustrate the nature of our hearts. We choose to protect and defend spiritual issues that are important and dear to us. We are loyal to certain sins and desires. We defend them against the conviction of the Spirit. But if we want to have victory, we must pull down the walls and expose the altars within our hearts that are dedicated to our own selfish lusts and immoral desires. Our altars are not wood or stone; they are electronic in nature. We bow before the electronic means of fueling our lust. We twist the goodness of grace into a means of supplying our sensual lusts. Jude 4 warns us of this pattern in the world: "ungodly people, who pervert the grace of our God into sensuality and deny our only Master and Lord, Jesus Christ." So we turn from the worship of God to the worship of our self-pleasure as our new lord.

In our hearts we have built an altar to sex that God is not allowed to take away. I say "altar" because we worship this desire. Worship? Yes. We have given it precedence over our allegiance to the King of kings and His worship. We are created to worship God, but instead we build altars to other gods, just as

Read Jeremiah 42–44. How foolish the people of Jeremiah's day were! But does our arrogance appear any less foolish?

_____

_____

_____

_____

_____

_____

Small groups: Discuss how you think we are equally proud in our thinking, setting ourselves up for failure.

_____

_____

_____

_____

_____

Talk to God about your tendency to be unwise in your life choices. Ask for His help. Then thank Him for the "light" that shone in your heart and changed your life.

_____

_____

_____

_____

_____

_____

_____

did the children of Israel. God destroyed Israel's physical enemies, but the people had to tear down their altars to false gods and build an altar to God alone. The greatest danger in the land was not its former occupants but rather the Canaanites' worship of false gods.

Take time to think long and hard about this concept. Meditate on the destruction that was caused by the idolatry that was allowed to enter the lives of God's people. Think about how calloused they became to the paganism in their lives that infected generation after generation of Israelites. A classic instance is found at the time of Jeremiah, when the people had just experienced the destruction of Jerusalem. Jeremiah bemoaned the loss of his city and its people, and was especially concerned over the lack of care shown by the people for what took place.

In Jeremiah 42–44 we read how a group of survivors came to Jeremiah, seemingly to hear from God as to what they should do next. God gave Jeremiah clear direction for these survivors. They ignored his words and God's instructions. Their reasoning reflected classic self-deception based on their blinded hearts and desires. They sought to get their way regardless of what Jeremiah said (and God's response shows that He knew they were proud and arrogant and would not hear anyway). Notice their idol-driven reasoning in 44:16–19; they say that, since they quit offering incense to the "queen of heaven," life has gone down the drain and they have been consumed (v. 18). They believe that if they just go down to Egypt and worship their gods there, all will be well. They are blinded by their own desire for things to go well, to have food, and "to be well." They do not believe that the war and famine will follow them there. What a joke! They have just watched people cannibalize their young and their enemies brutalize their families. Now they think it is God's fault or because of Jeremiah's wrong counsel that they are in this trouble. The "queen of heaven" will take care of them.

This is how deceived a sensual idolater will become. Such a person is fully persuaded that enjoying the flesh is acceptable and good for his or her life. Idolaters will not accept that God must judge this sinful lifestyle. They are convinced that they can go ahead with their fleshly desires and worship their sensual pleasures.

Note
1 **Fanny Crosby,** 1890.

Day 5. Understand the Promises and Dangers

Daily Meditation Themes

- *Goodness of God:* "Sing to God, sing praises to his name ... exult before him! ... Blessed be the Lord, who daily bears us up" (Ps. 68:4, 19). "For God, who said, 'Let light shine out of darkness,' has shone in our hearts to give the light of the knowledge of the glory of God in the face of Jesus Christ" (2 Cor. 4:6).

- *Greatness of God:* "Fear not; for I am with you; be not dismayed, for I am your God" (Isa. 41:10). "'For I am the LORD your God, the Holy One of Israel ... I am he: before me no God was formed ... you are my witnesses,' declares the LORD, 'and I am God'" (43:3, 10, 12). "Thus says the LORD, the King of Israel and his Redeemer, the LORD of hosts: 'I am the first and I am the last; besides me there is no god'" (44:6). "I am the LORD, and there is no other, besides me there is no God; I equip you, though you do not know me ... For thus says the LORD, who created the heavens (he is God!), who formed the earth and made it (he established it; he did not create it empty, he formed it to be inhabited!): 'I am the LORD, and there is no other ... Turn to me and be saved, all the ends of the earth! For I am God, and there is no other'" (45:5, 18, 22). "Remember the former things of old: for I am God, and there is no other; I am God, and there is none like me" (46:9). "I am the LORD your God who stirs up the sea so that its waves roar—the LORD of hosts is his name" (51:15).

Meditate on these passages and consider God's greatness. What do you see?

_____
_____
_____
_____
_____
_____
_____
_____
_____
_____
_____
_____
_____
_____
_____
_____
_____
_____
_____
_____
_____
_____
_____
_____
_____
_____
_____
_____

Think about God's grace. Explain it and illustrate it to yourself. Now ask yourself this question: When does grace no longer seem amazing?

_____
_____
_____
_____
_____
_____
_____
_____
_____
_____
_____
_____
_____
_____
_____
_____
_____
_____
_____
_____
_____
_____
_____
_____
_____
_____
_____
_____

Song: "Amazing Grace"

Amazing grace! How sweet the sound
That saved a wretch like me!
I once was lost, but now am found;
Was blind, but now I see.

'Twas grace that taught my heart to fear,
And grace my fears relieved;
How precious did that grace appear
The hour I first believed.

Grace came to man in human form,
From sin to set us free!
Grace took our shame, broken and torn,
To pay sin's penalty.

Grace shed the blood of Christ that day;
In giving He must die;
The Father turned His face away,
"It's finished!" Grace did cry.

Through many dangers, toils, and snares,
I have already come;
'Tis grace hath brought me safe thus far,
And grace will lead me home.

The Lord has promis'd good to me,
His word my hope secures;
He will my shield and portion be,
As long as life endures.

Yes, when this flesh and heart shall fail,
And mortal life shall cease,
I shall possess, within the veil,
A life of joy and peace.

When we've been there ten thousand years,
Bright shining as the sun,
We've no less days to sing God's praise
Than when we first begun.[1]

Meditation

Read 1 Corinthians 10:12–13. This short passage comes at the end of a section where Paul has referred to historical events in the history of Israel that should be examples to us of what failure, sin, rebellion, and immorality look like. Paul suggests two responses to facing these kinds of temptations.

The first response is that of arrogance and pride (v. 12). "I can handle this. I know what kind of sin this is and how to overcome it. I don't need accountability or protections. I know the Internet and other electronic media. I'm fine. Don't worry about me. I have never lost a battle of the mind and morals yet." This person is set up for a major fall which will have cataclysmic results. It will take only one carefully placed moral choice in the minefield of sin to blow his or her arrogant self out of ministry, family, and respectability. To those in this group Paul says, "Take heed."

Others who are open to this tendency toward pride are those who have had a measure of victory. These victors think that they have conquered their lust. The flesh is no problem to them, so they say. They too will crash and burn.

The second response when facing temptation is that of defeat and expected failure (v. 13). Many people choose to go into moral failure regularly. They have no idea how they can get out of this pattern of deceit, covering sin, deep shame, and sensual enslavement. To those in this group Paul says, "Take hope." Many have faced similar temptations and even worse but have retained their integrity, spirituality, and humility. The humble person expects temptation and relies daily on the Spirit for help to escape it successfully. Humble sinners who walk in God's grace can be greatly encouraged by the focus on God in this verse. God knows and cares about our individual tests. His purpose is to grow us in grace. We can walk

Memorize 1 Corinthians 10:13. Write it out for yourself, making it personal. For example, write "No temptation has overtaken ME ..."

by faith in all of God's power and none of our own. But don't say, "I can't do it." The weight of sin and temptation is not too much for God's grace. Push through it in Christ. Ignore any thoughts of failure. Trust Christ to help.

Notice several encouraging things Paul says to you as a former "loser" who is to be an overcomer.

First, you are not alone. Many others have faced the same kinds of temptations. So keep your perspective. Don't let self or Satan put you on a trip to a pity party. Life really is a great event when God is involved.

Second, God is faithful. Repeat it! Write it! Believe it! God is faithful! Don't ever forget it.

He knows exactly what you can handle and He wants you to succeed. When you think you hit a spiritual wall that is too high, and that is the reason for your failure, remember that God believed that you could successfully negotiate that temptation by His grace. He will help you find a way through it. Always.

Third, you are never alone. God provides a way for you to go *through* the test of your heart. He wants you to be true to His holiness. He wants you to love and worship Him and find your satisfaction in Him.

Note

1 **John Newton,** 1779; vv. 3–4 by **Dave Coats.**

Day 6. Practical Help for the Battle

Daily Meditation Themes

- *Goodness of God:* "May all who seek you rejoice and be glad in you! May those who love your salvation say evermore, 'God is great!'" (Ps. 70:4). "For it is all for your sake, so that as grace extends to more and more people it may increase thanksgiving, to the glory of God" (2 Cor. 4:15).
- *Greatness of God:* "Thus shall you say to them: 'The gods who did not make the heavens and the earth shall perish from the earth and from under the heavens.' It is he who made the earth by his power, who established the world by his wisdom, and by his understanding stretched out the heavens" (Jer. 10:11–12).

Song: "Soldiers of Christ, Arise"

Soldiers of Christ, arise, and put your armor on,
Strong in the strength which God supplies through
  His eternal Son.
Strong in the Lord of hosts, and in His mighty power,
Who in the strength of Jesus trusts is more
  than conqueror.

Stand then in His great might, with all His
  strength endued,
But take, to arm you for the fight, the panoply of
  God;
That, having all things done, and all your conflicts
  passed,
Ye may o'ercome through Christ alone and stand
  entire at last.

Leave no unguarded place, no weakness of the soul,
Take every virtue, every grace, and fortify the whole;
Indissolubly joined, to battle all proceed;
But arm yourselves with all the mind that was in
  Christ, your Head.[1]

Meditation on God:

What kind of love is this?

69

Example of Journaling

(There is a starter journal in Appendix 4.)

Monday: *I had a good day. This was expected because yesterday I heard a great message that really helped me start the week well. I was "pumped" about doing well.*

Tuesday: *I lost some of the emotion today. I was somewhat sloppy about my personal disciplines and dependence on God. I did OK until I spent time just hanging out and then took a nap in the afternoon. I was kind of tired and so I found that I was in a mood for giving in to selfish/sensual thoughts. I just wasn't in the mood for fighting this today.*

Wednesday: *I looked back at the trend so far and realized that I was trying to build my spiritual success off my emotions and how I feel. I have to plow through regardless of how I feel. I took time to review the truth of Romans 6–8.*

Thursday: *I committed myself to better memory work to help keep myself thinking about my daily walk and temptations the way God wants me to. My weakest area is thinking about my times off (weekends, evenings when I don't have studies, vacations). Then I'm most focused on self. So I need to deny self and think on what it means to follow Christ. He took the cross. What have I really done for Him? I have never resisted "to the point of shedding [my] blood" like Christ did (Heb. 12:2–4).*

Friday: *I had a very good day in Christ. My new focus is to spend time every morning thinking about God. I know this is not normal.*

Meditation

Now that we have looked at these four passages (Rom. 6–8; Gal. 5:16–26; 2 Cor. 10:4–5; 1 Cor. 10:12–13), let me give you two practical suggestions for building upon the biblical material. The Bible material is critical: without it you will only be doing reformation of life, which is a work anyone can do. Only a believer can by faith trust what God tells us about the battle. However, once a believer has the biblical foundation, he or she can use the following tools to help fight the battle.

1. JOURNALING YOUR STRUGGLE

It is vitally important that you identify practically the patterns of sin you have set up in your life. You have disguised and allowed sinful, fleshly patterns for years or at least months. Now God says it is time for you to pay attention to the details of a life that leads to sin.

If you are going to be serious and deal practically with the problem, you will need to get hold of a simple notebook in which you can write down your thoughts, including those at the times when you struggle. Perhaps the best way to do this is as part of the daily journal you keep of your thoughts when you study God's Word. Alternatively, use a separate sheet of paper and take time daily to note what steps led to your failure. This will help you change your thinking, avoid certain places, and change certain habits that lead to sensuality. Don't procrastinate. Commit to writing, at least once a day, a brief history of your struggles and temptations.

I especially appreciate Paul Tripp's helpful five-step Q & A that unpacks what goes on in a moment of temptation. Question one, what is the situation? It includes all of the surrounding circumstances that are out of your control. The circumstances just are a reality. Question two, what are you thinking? You face the temptation.

Do you think, "who cares?" Or what do you think? Question three, what do you do? What process do you go through to get what you want? Question four, what is your desire at that moment? What do you want? A brief pleasure? A quick fix? Question five, what is the result? Do you see the trend?

One young man who was coming out of pornography and sensual relationships still struggled at times with holding a right view of women. I challenged him to write in his journal every time he found himself sitting on our campus just watching people come and go. He came back the next week and told me that he found himself naturally assessing each girl who came in the door. He then related his thoughts about each girl and her attraction to

Normal is looking/thinking first about me, not God. This really was good.

Saturday: I slept in and did not keep my commitment to thinking first on God. I got up and jumped into a project rather than taking time to meditate on Christ and the cross. I gave in to masturbation today. Failure.

Sunday: No problems. When I sat down and looked back at the week, overall there is a lot for me to rejoice in what God is showing me. I must move forward in this battle and follow Christ to victory.

him. He found himself doing things to get certain girls' attention so that they would notice him. He would also fantasize that he was the "macho" guy they were looking for. Such thoughts sound foolish when written down, but a whole realm of thought processes were unearthed through his journal. This helped start the process of changing his thought patterns, desires, lusts, and actions toward holy, righteous, and godly actions. Change must take place in the reality of everyday life.

2. PRAYER TARGET

Satan is out to attack us in every way possible. He will find out by trial and error (he is not omniscient) what our weak spots are in our lives. Then he attacks. He sends his means of attracting our interests, arousing our desires, and confusing our thoughts. If we are not aware of this, we will fall flat on our spiritual faces in the mud of despair and failure. We will feel that we can never overcome the flesh and the devil. Yet Ephesians 6:10–18 explains that we are equipped to defend ourselves and fight back, if we prepare well. First Peter 5:8 reminds us that we are being stalked by the "lion" who would devour us.

Paul's first letter to the Corinthians contains a great word of hope for us. He writes that we can and should be victorious over temptation (1 Cor. 10:13). But along with the other tools for helping us get back on track spiritually, there is one means of quickly getting our focus away from the cheap allurements of the world and back to God, where our focus should always be. Not only should we have a practice of meditating on the glory of God, but we should also be ready to turn the attack back on Satan's fortress. Think of this process in terms of a military battle. If you are on the defensive, in self-protection mode, in your fortress, you do no real damage to the enemy. So you must go on the offensive. If Satan attacks your worship of

Small groups: Share with one another how "journaling" helps you in the battle for a pure heart. Write down your thoughts here:

_____

_____

_____

_____

_____

_____

_____

_____

_____

_____

_____

Are we able to imagine what it meant that Christ took the curse for us? Can we fathom the reality of His being made a curse for those who would not hear and would not accept His salvation? He died even for the atheists and the agnostics.

_____

_____

_____

_____

_____

_____

_____

_____

_____

_____

God through the temptation to lust, return fire immediately. Be in the offensive mode. One way to go on the offensive is to pray for those who are lost: seek God intensely for their souls.

You should have a list of a few people who are lost and who are close to your heart. These are the folk that you pray for regularly, probably weekly, in the hope that God will draw them to Himself in salvation. So, when Satan next attacks you and tries to get you to relax the purity of your mind, go immediately into prayer for one of those lost people. Make a determined appeal to God on this person's behalf and for his or her soul. *This prayer tool is not a gimmick. You must pray this way with a sincere heart and genuine concern for the lost.* In fact, if you do not know how fervently to seek God's ear for someone's eternal soul, pleading that his or her heart's door will swing wide open to the good news, you can save your breath, especially if it is just a "courtesy prayer."

Below is a list of Scripture verses, in New Testament order, that may motivate you to build a good prayer life for lost folk. We must pray fervently and biblically for their condition and eternal state. Satan will not like this offensive attack at all. As you work your way through the New Testament, recognize the theological description of the condition of the lost person and of the dramatic work God has done. I hope you will find other verses or passages that help your heart grow in its sense of gratefulness to God.

PRAYING FOR LOST PEOPLE

Sin's road ends in destruction	Matthew 7:13
The way to life is narrow	Matthew 7:14
We must believe in Jesus as our Savior	John 1:12
The lost will perish	John 3:16
Christ died for their sins	John 3:16
They are condemned already	John 3:18

They love darkness not light	John 3:19
They must be born again	John 3:7
The wrath of God remains on those who do not repent	John 3:36
The Father draws all people to Him	John 6:44
They must know God	John 17:3
They must repent because of God's goodness	Romans 2:4
God's wrath is coming	Romans 2:5
No one seeks God	Romans 3:11
God's glory is too high for us to attain	Romans 3:23
Christ died for the ungodly	Romans 5:6
Christ died for us	Romans 5:8
God loves sinners	Romans 5:8
Sin requires a death penalty	Romans 6:23
It is God who shows mercy	Romans 9:16
Preaching the cross is foolish	1 Corinthians 1:20–25
The gospel is veiled from sinners	2 Corinthians 4:3
Satan blinds minds	2 Corinthians 4:4
Without Christ we "fail to meet the test"	2 Corinthians 13:5–6
Christ became a curse for the lost	Galatians 3:13
Forgiveness of sins is needed	Ephesians 1:7
People are dead in their sins	Ephesians 2:1
By nature we are children of wrath	Ephesians 2:3
We are enemies of God	Ephesians 2:14–16
Man's understanding is darkened	Ephesians 4:18
The lost world is deceived	Titus 3:3
Judgment is certain	Hebrews 9:27
There's no second chance	Hebrews 9:27
Vengeance belongs to God; he will repay	Hebrews 10:30
It is a fearful thing to be judged by God	Hebrews 10:31
We must have the Son of God	1 John 5:12
Eternity is long	Revelation 20:10
Hell is real	Revelation 21:8

Spend a moment in thanksgiving to God for His goodness to you. The truth of these verses applied to you once upon a time—and then the gospel changed everything. Consider what God has done to redeem you from your sins: you were once His enemy; you were not seeking God; you did not want to accept the truth; you were arrogantly and rebelliously living your own life and foolish enough to think you could somehow do OK with God. Then He made you His child and brought you near.

Write out how you will use this prayer-target idea. For example:

I know that I tend to be hit by temptation in the morning when I don't get up straight away. If thoughts from my sensual past start coming into my mind, I have my prayer list of lost people memorized so that I can go directly to intercession.

_____
_____
_____
_____
_____
_____
_____
_____
_____
_____
_____
_____
_____

Here is an example of what prayer for your lost friend could be like.

Dear God, I know that sin requires a penalty of death. I know that this includes my uncle. He is a sinner and has rejected You for over seventy years. He has nothing to recommend himself to You. So I know he deserves that pain and separation of death, and hell. But I also know that You have given him the opportunity at times to hear about the cross. You have said that preaching the cross is foolishness, but it is also the power of God. I am counting on this power of the cross to reach his heart with his need of salvation.

Small groups: Share who is on your "prayer-target" list and why.

Note

1 **Charles Wesley** (1707–1788). Public domain.

Day 7. Focus on the Cross

This week we move to the fireside time with Peter in Matthew 26:69–75. Consider what it is like for Peter to be there. What are some of his fears and struggles as the people confront him and he begins to deny the Lord? Put yourself in his place and realize that all the times when you have turned away from Christ to find satisfaction in the cheap pleasures of this world of sensuality, you too would have had no desire to identify with Christ and face persecution and execution. Feel the shame as Peter knows the eyes of Christ have found and seen him there, denying his connection with the Son of God. Run with him as Peter tries to get away from the horrible scene that will play out in his mind many times. He will see over and over the torn beard, the beaten face, and the spittle on the body of his Lord and Master. For Peter, the long night and the next days will seem an eternity as he lives with a conscience and mind that accuse him of the worst act of betrayal. Judas had turned traitor, but Peter was one of the disciples with whom Christ had spent the most time and to whom he had given the best opportunities to know Him and be close to Him. In that moment of denial, and over the next days, Peter cannot help but relive the last couple of years and the discipleship work of Christ invested in him personally. The shame of not being willing to stand for and with his Master/Teacher runs very deep.

Daily Meditation Theme

- *Greatness of God:* "Not to us, O LORD, not to us, but to your name give glory, for the sake of your steadfast love and your faithfulness! … Our God is in the

Meditation: when you spend time thinking about and expressing the work of God, do not allow this to become a ritual. Use worship and praise to lift your heart to heaven.

Focus on the cross. How frail we are as humans. How selfish and self-preserving are our lives. We cannot even seem to allow the greatness and magnitude of the glory of God to change our shallow attempts at finding pleasure.

75

Which part of these first two weeks do you need to review? Write down which verses or passages you need to put into your weekly review so that they are strong in your memory.

_____

_____

_____

_____

_____

_____

_____

Small groups: Has one particular Day 7 focus been a particular help to you? Why? Discuss this in your group.

_____

_____

_____

_____

_____

_____

Do today's songs help you boast in the cross? How does this happen for you?

_____

_____

_____

_____

_____

_____

_____

_____

heavens; he does all that he pleases" (Ps. 115:1, 3).

Song 1: "The Gospel Song"

Holy God, in love, became
Perfect Man to bear my blame
On the cross He took my sin
By His death I live again.[1]

Song 2: "Be Unto Your Name"

We are a moment, You are forever;
Lord of the Ages, God before time.
We are a vapor, You are eternal;
Love everlasting reigning on high.

Holy, Holy, Lord God Almighty!
Worthy is the Lamb who was slain.
Highest praises, honor and glory,
Be unto Your name, be unto Your name.

We are the broken, You are the Healer;
Jesus, Redeemer, mighty to save.
You are the love song we'll sing forever;
Bowing before You, blessing Your name.[2]

Notes

1 Bob Kauflin. © 2002 Sovereign Grace Worship (ASCAP)/Sovereign Grace Praise (BMI). www.SovereignGraceMusic.org. Used with permission.

2 Gary Sadler. Lynn DeShazo. © 1998 Integrity's Hosanna! Music.

Before We Go Further ...

At this point it is critical to address the struggle you may have had with the meditation themes and to encourage you in your patterns so far. Hardly a week goes by when I am not meeting with someone with whom I need to explain again the priority and necessity for this daily work. I know that it takes time to grow and become accustomed to this part of your walk with God, but nothing else, and nothing less, will do.

Let me explain it this way. Psalm 1:2 says that the man who is blessed in his daily life is the one who delights in the "law of the LORD." It is this Word that the blessed man meditates on day and night. So when do we reach this "blessed" stage? How do we get there? How do "delight" and "meditate" chorus together and cause us to be changed for God's glory? We have to start doing it. Doing what? Meditating. We can't gain delight until we start thinking on it and enjoying what God says. We can't enjoy what God says until we gain a delight in what we know already. It is a cycle of reading, thinking, desiring, and responding in joy to God's character and work. Until you apply what God says about Himself to your life today and enjoy the fruit of God's goodness and grace, you will not delight in God and His Word. This is what Psalm 37:4 also says: "Delight yourself in the LORD." So begin to enjoy or delight in God's righteousness, His holiness, His goodness, His purity, His majesty, and His love—to name just a few attributes. How? By seeing how these attributes have been used for your benefit and for your salvation. Meditate on what your life would be like without this kind of God at work. You cannot begin to thank Him enough for His good works and His great love for you. Think about what it means that God made the universe. You read about stars and galaxies that are three billion light-years away and in wonder see how that demonstrates an incredible, immense God. And you are His child. You are His interest, His investment, and His love. Can you not delight in Him? Are you starting to get the picture? Now God fulfills Psalm 37:4 by giving you your heart desires—the things that you want. You want God to change the desires of your heart to His holy ones.

What is the difference between this meditation and memorization? How can someone who has memorized ten trillion verses in a children's program, Christian school, Christian college, or seminary go out and live an ungodly life? How can a pastor who preaches the Bible have pornography downloaded onto his laptop? This does not seem to add up. Well, such a person could be lost. For Christians, however, we can store all kinds of information in our brains for future retrieval, as necessary, but in order for the truth to change us, we must allow it to enter our meditations and the desires of our hearts, not just leave it to reside in our brains. Keeping truth only in the brain is an explanation for why kids in Christian homes can be so ungrateful, even when they have been given so much. They live out Romans 2:4, despising the rich goodness of God. The good thing about memory, however, is that it allows you to retrieve the truth, think on it, delight in it, and apply it to your day, your

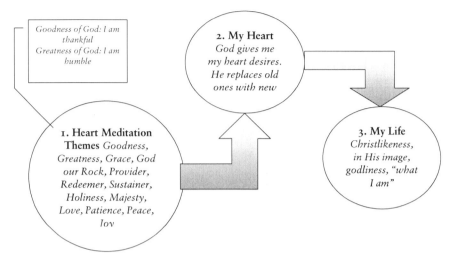

work, your marriage, and your troubles. This process is *meditation*, and meditation leads to enjoyment or delight in what God has said. The diagram shows why verse memorization by itself fails to "connect" with the heart.

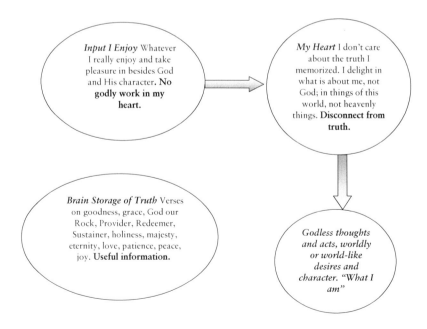

Week 3.
Protect the Heart

Do not allow yourself to take trips back into the cesspool of sensuality.

We have now reset the conscience correctly. We have taken time to look at the biblical foundations for fighting this war against sensual lust and desire. Now we need to specifically target the heart. We saw in Week 1 that the heart is under attack. It is the battleground on which the war of purity is waged. Therefore the scriptural admonitions that we will look at this week need to be heard.

Day 1. Flee! (1)

Daily Meditation Themes

- *Goodness of God:* "I will remember the deeds of the LORD; yes, I will remember your wonders of old. I will ponder all your work, and meditate on your mighty deeds" (Ps. 77:11–12). "And he died for all, that those who live might no longer live for themselves but for him who for their sake died and was raised" (2 Cor. 5:15).
- *Greatness of God:* "The LORD says to my Lord: 'Sit at my right hand, until I make your enemies your footstool'" (Ps. 110:1).

Song: "Bow the Knee"

What a privilege to come into God's presence,
Just to linger with the One who set me free.
As I lift my eyes and see His awesome glory,
I remember who He is and bow the knee.

Bow the knee, bow the knee,
He is King of all the ages, bow the knee!
God alone, on His throne,
See Him high and lifted up and bow the knee!
Kneel before Him, all adore Him.
As you live to love Him more, bow the knee.

In His hand He holds the power of creation.
With His voice He spoke and all things came to be.
Yet He hears each simple prayer I bring before Him,
When I humbly seek His face and bow the knee.[1]

Meditation

There will be times when you will need to *flee.* You should not see this as prompted by fear of man. In order to avoid falling into sin and temptation, you must know what to do when you find yourself in a vulnerable moment and place. Most of us who struggle with impure thoughts find that Satan knows how to send

80

waves of temptation our way. Paul's admonition to the Corinthian believers was to "Flee from sexual immorality" (1 Cor. 6:18)—to turn away from it, because the body is God's (v. 13). He knew their background (vv. 9–11), and he knew that some of them had come out of homosexuality, adultery, and other forms of immorality. But now that they were "washed" and "sanctified," these things belonged to their past. They were to flee them.

Imagine one of those church members going into Corinth for her daily work and walking down through the district where she used to work as a temple prostitute. Or here's another member who knows the area just off the marketplace in Corinth, which has ready access to all kinds of filth of the flesh. Do these folk tempt themselves by putting themselves in moral danger? No. They avoid those areas and those people. If someone from their past lives tries to drag them back into those things, they run. Literally.

But here is Bill in Chicago, and he struggles with the temptation to look at porn DVDs; or Mark, who can't seem to get the images from his last Internet hook-up out of his mind; or Sue, who is trying to leave behind her cell phone addiction to sensuality. They must all make some serious decisions to obey God's command to flee the things that draw them back into their idolatry at the altar of sensuality.

Note

1 **Ron Hamilton and Cheryl Reid.** ©2004 by Majesty Music, Inc. All rights reserved. Used by permission.

Write out what "fleeing" would look like for you.

Small groups: If you don't flee lust, what will be the result? Imagine that Joseph had given in to Potiphar's wife (Gen. 39). What would have happened then? David did not flee his temptation (2 Sam. 11). What came of his not fleeing?

Day 2. Flee! (2)

Dave: *I remember as a teen going to a major library in Minneapolis for the first time. I had no idea that I had parked in a major hooker district, one block away from the library (I was sheltered!). But when I realized where I was, you can believe that I got moving. I would do the same thing with my remote control or my computer mouse. No time to linger in a dangerous area.*

Daily Meditation Themes

- *Goodness of God:* "He has caused his wondrous works to be remembered; the LORD is gracious and merciful" (Ps. 111:4).
- *Greatness of God:* "I will ponder all your work, and meditate on your mighty deeds. Your way, O God, is holy. What god is great like our God?" (Ps. 77:12–13); "There is none like you among the gods, O Lord, nor are there any works like yours. All the nations you have made shall come and worship before you, O Lord, and shall glorify your name. For you are great and do wondrous things; you alone are God" (86:8–10).

Song: "Worthy of Worship"

Worthy of worship, worthy of praise,
Worthy of honor and glory;
Worthy of all the glad songs we can sing,
Worthy of all of the off'rings we bring.

You are worthy, Father, Creator,
You are worthy, Saviour, Sustainer,
You are worthy, worthy and wonderful;
Worthy of worship and praise.

Worthy of rev'rence, worthy of fear,
Worthy of love and devotion;
Worthy of bowing and bending of knees,
Worthy of all this and added to these.

Almighty Father, Master and Lord,
King of all kings and Redeemer;
Wonderful Counselor, Comforter, Friend,
Saviour, and Source of our life without end.[1]

Meditation

So that you do not feel that I see the command by Paul in his epistles to flee as an unnecessary detour spiritually or as a point that Paul really did not need to make, let's take another day to bring this home by looking at his mention of the same point in 2 Timothy 2. This is Paul's last letter before he goes to glory, so he does not waste time writing unnecessary things. Yet he exhorts Timothy, his son in the faith, about a carefulness of life and ministry as he leads the church body (2:15–26).

Part of Paul's concern is that Timothy be a proper vessel, pure and useful for the Master (vv. 20–21); therefore he should depart from iniquity, as should everyone who names the name of Christ (v. 19). Part of this separation from sin is to flee the lusts of youth (v. 22) and to follow righteousness. Paul is reinforcing his "put off," "put on" theme. He never thinks that just one or the other is enough in itself.

Notice too that Paul's admonition is connected with a reminder to join with others who are serving God out of a "pure heart" (v. 22). Such a friendship of purity and encouragement among believers in their joint pursuit of a holy life is very helpful. Take time with others to pray together about your desire to follow Christ and to flee lust.

One of the things that we need to do in our churches and youth groups is to build a healthy love among the members of the body of Christ. In Ephesians 4 Paul uses the body metaphor to help us understand that growing into Christlikeness is a group activity. We need one another. There is a whole group of texts in the New Testament that explain what God expects of our relationships with one another. The activity God expects and commands the most is loving one another. This *agapé* love is a self-sacrificial love that expects nothing in return. When we are willing to love one another self-sacrificially, we will desire to help one another change and become more pure and holy, like our God.

Small groups: How do you think the older ones in your group can admonish the younger ones? What dangers can older people recognize that young people might not?

Getting involved in body life is one of the most needed and yet neglected parts of the church today. I assume it has always been somewhat difficult for people to crush their pride and to humble themselves before others. But this is what God calls us to in the body of Christ through His church. People get hurt and they close up. They feel vulnerable and they are uncomfortable. But 1 Corinthians 13:4–7 love calls us to respond differently to one another in Christ. When we settle for something less than this picture of being followers of Christ, we lose some of the most vital activity in the New Testament.

Note
1 **Blankenship and York.** Copyright 1988 by McKinney Music, Inc.

Day 3. Think on These Things Daily!

Daily Meditation Themes

- *Goodness of God:* "If God is for us, who can be against us? He who did not spare his own Son but gave him up for us all, how will he not also with him graciously give us all things?" (Rom. 8:31–32).
- *Greatness of God:* "Do you not fear me? declares the LORD; do you not tremble before me? I placed the sand as the boundary for the sea, a perpetual barrier that it cannot pass; though the waves toss, they cannot prevail; though they roar, they cannot pass over it" (Jer. 5:22).

Song: "And Can It Be"

And can it be that I should gain
An int'rest in the Savior's blood?
Died He for me, who caused His pain—
For me, who Him to death pursued?
Amazing love! How can it be
That thou, my God, shouldst die for me?

He left His Father's throne above,
So free, so infinite His grace,
Humbled Himself and came in love,
And bled for Adam's helpless race.
'Tis mercy all, immense and free,
For O my God, it found out me!

No condemnation now I dread,
Jesus, and all in Him, is mine;
Alive in Him, my living Head,
And clothed in righteousness divine,
Bold I approach the eternal throne
And claim the crown, through Christ my own.[1]

Meditation

I remember once visiting in a home while traveling. The son was vacuuming, but the

---

What do you see in your God?

Can you comprehend the sacrifice of Christ as He left heaven?

Small groups: We are not trying to be legalists. Standards exist only to help us with obedience to God. Not watching certain movies or not visiting certain Web sites does not make us pure. These standards are fences of protection. We can call them fences of love. What application from this can you make for yourself? Be specific.

_____
_____
_____
_____
_____
_____
_____
_____
_____
_____
_____
_____
_____
_____
_____
_____
_____
_____
_____
_____
_____
_____
_____
_____

vacuum cleaner had a problem. It would work for about five minutes and then stop. He would open it up and shut it with a bang, after which it would work for another five minutes. I asked him to let me see the inside of the cleaner. The bag and its filter were full and clogged, yet he was content to work this way, hampered by a dirty machine that would have worked so much better if it had been cleaned. That is what our hearts are like. They need cleansing and clearing through by the Word and meditating on God's beauty and glory. We should not be content to live our lives with hearts that are constantly struggling with filth.

You cannot afford to be lax concerning the input into your heart. The heart is the source of your life desires and decisions. Take the Philippians 4:8 challenge: "Finally, brothers, whatever is true, whatever is honorable, whatever is just, whatever is pure, whatever is lovely, whatever is commendable, if there is any excellence, if there is anything worthy of praise, think about these things." Filter everything you hear, see, and do through this verse. It is like the filter on your Internet access, cutting out that which is not acceptable to God. Filter your music, movies, and other entertainment through this set of guidelines. Satan wants to get kids hooked on sensuality early. Students I talk to often speak of their first influences or exposure to some level of immorality and pornography having come at the age of eight, ten, or twelve years old.

If you are an older Christian, you need to help younger Christians realize what kinds of things they are exposing themselves to that are not wise. Along with youth goes a lack of experience. This immaturity leads to a laxity and a casualness that are dangerous. Help younger Christians put up their guard. Show them the principles and explain what the long-term effects will be if they don't filter out the world's filth. This is God's command: it is not optional. I am especially concerned about homes in which the parents exercise little or no leadership in this area.

Let's be honest: part of our problem is our laxness about what we regard as "OK" for consumption. If someone asks you what you watch or look at, you think you are doing fine. Be specific: how sensual are the clothes the women wear? Are the lead people in the programs you watch moving toward pure and permanent relationships, or temporary and immoral ones? When your favorite programs laugh at purity or show "making out" to be the norm, you are setting yourself up for heart attitudes that are not pure and beautiful.

Proverbs 4:23 says, "Keep your heart with all vigilance." The image the writer gives us is of a soldier on guard over a restricted area. He has been given the solemn responsibility of keeping people out of this place. The heart is to be so guarded, for out of the heart come all the situations, problems, choices, and desires of life.

One thing we must address is the "toys or tools" approach to life. Let me apply this to the Internet; you can make the application to all other areas of your audio/video intake.

For most of us who need to address our online purity, our main problem is this: *we use the Internet as a toy, not a tool. We use it for entertainment rather than for edification.* We cannot afford to do this. We think we can handle it, but we are foolish to think so. Let's be wise and understanding in how to use the Internet. Satan knows that he can use certain times, our responsibilities, the flesh, and our tiredness to open doors of temptation.

What does it mean to use the Internet for entertainment rather than for edification? *Why is the former more likely to lead us into temptation?*

Remember that your heart is *deceptive*. You will tend to look at things less critically when your heart enjoys what it sees or gets caught up in it. For movie lovers, you get into the story and have a hard time turning off a good story line, even if it is sensual. For "gamers," you are intoxicated and enamored by your success in the game and you ignore the deadening effects the graphics and music have on you.

Do you think you need help in removing certain influences? Who can help you radically cut off certain areas of input to your heart? Discuss this in your small groups. Help one another.

_____
_____
_____
_____
_____
_____

Which influence do you find hardest to deal with? Why?

_____
_____
_____
_____
_____
_____

Do you recognize the steps that take you toward failure? List them and keep them visible.

_____
_____
_____
_____
_____
_____
_____

Small groups: Pray for one another in your weakness.

WE WANT TO BE ENTERTAINED RATHER THAN USE IT TO DO RESEARCH

We may not go on the Internet initially to view sensual images or pornography, but they are there. Once we run across them, we are tempted to go back again.

TYPES OF SITES
- Game sites: they provide the opportunity of going into all kinds of pornography
- Picture sites: these contain amateur porn or worse
- Movie, video clip, and Hollywood sites: these lead to, or contain, bad images and sensuality
- Sports sites: many of us are attracted to sensual pictures of the cheerleaders which border on pornography
- Auction sites: if we don't go in with specific goals and get out as soon as we have met those goals, we will see things that draw us in where we should not go

OUR ATTITUDES
- We tend not to be in a spiritually directed mode; we are in a *self-pleasing mode.*
- We tend to be in a "surf and cruise" mode, landing wherever we feel like going.
- We tend to go wherever our eyes and senses take us.
- We tend to have our temptation defenses down when we are "hanging out" online.
- We tend to just chat, talk, and look for cool things to see and play.
- We spend long periods of time in temporal pursuit (things that do not last for eternity).
- We feel that it won't hurt to look at a few moderately sensual pictures. After all, we don't have a problem with this with DVDs and movies. A swimsuit, bikini, model, actress, or other picture is something we enjoy looking at. We don't see the harm.

We like Googling our favorite movie celebrity and seeing what is going on in his or her life. We find ourselves looking at that person's latest movie clips and still photos. These pictures tend to be pretty revealing or sensual.

WHAT IS IT LIKE TO BE ONLINE WITH PURPOSE?

- We go to a specific site or we do a specific search. *Sports:* we go and check the score and get out. *Video sites:* we want to see the latest funny stuff that we can send to our friends or we want to view what someone sends us. Don't do it. It's not worth it. *Auctions:* we know what we're looking for. Check it off and then get out.
- We have specific parameters for where we will go online.
- We watch out for the traps and allurements that advertisers send out to draw us into sensuality.
- When doing searches on Google or elsewhere, we ignore or block any sidebar advertisements.
- We are careful what we enter into search engines. We know exactly what we are seeking. If we get into something that is off-limits, we get out of it immediately.
- We use the tool of the Internet to accomplish ministry and life tasks, not enjoying it as an entertainment center for the flesh. Following the lives of the "rich and famous" is something that diverts our attention away from a faith-based, heavenly focus.
- We use it as a tool for eternity, not as a place to waste the time God gives us. We are conscious of the time we have and we are aware that we can easily spend hours on games and entertainment.

Note

1 **Charles Wesley,** 1738; altered wording in v. 2 by Majesty Hymns. Copyright 1997 by Majesty Music, Inc., Greenville, SC.

Day 4. Amputate! (1)

Greatness of God: What do you see?

_____
_____
_____
_____
_____
_____
_____
_____
_____
_____
_____
_____
_____
_____

How does this song minister to an immoral heart?

_____
_____
_____
_____
_____
_____
_____
_____
_____
_____
_____
_____
_____
_____
_____
_____
_____
_____

Daily Meditation Themes

- *Goodness of God:* "I will sing of the steadfast love of the LORD, forever" (Ps. 89:1). "All this is from God, who through Christ reconciled us to himself and gave us the ministry of reconciliation" (2 Cor. 5:18).
- *Greatness of God:* "When he utters his voice, there is a tumult of waters in the heavens, and he makes the mist rise from the ends of the earth. He makes lightning for the rain, and he brings forth the wind from his storehouses" (Jer. 10:13).

Song: "How Can It Be?"

O Savior, as my eyes behold
The wonders of Thy might untold,
The heav'ns in glorious light arrayed,
The vast creation Thou hast made—
And yet to think Thou lovest me—
My heart cries out, "How can it be?"

How can it be? How can it be?
That God should love a soul like me,
O how can it be?

As at the cross I humbly bow
And gaze upon Thy thorn-crowned brow,
And view the precious bleeding form
By cruel nails so bruised and torn,
To know Thy suff'ring was for me,
In grief I cry, "How can it be?"

How can it be? How can it be?
Was ever grace so full and free!
From heights of bliss to depths of woe
In loving kindness Thou didst go,
From sin and shame to rescue me—
O Love Divine, How can it be?[1]

Meditation

Today and tomorrow we will be looking at what we call the "amputation" of spiritual wickedness that infects our lives. Radical amputation means putting off what is sin and putting on what is right. In Colossians 3:5 Paul says that we are to put to death the following activities that affect our bodies: "sexual immorality, impurity, passion, evil desire … idolatry." These are things that we have engaged in but which we must now "put off" (v. 9). Decide which category listed in verse 5 your struggle falls into.

Using Colossians 3:1–4, find the basis for moving on to heavenly things. This passage closely parallels Romans 6. Our minds and desires are to be set on heavenly things so that we can cut off the old, sensual habits and longings. Ask yourself, "Am I really, passionately seeking the things above, or do I still desire the things of this world? Is that part of my continued struggle?" If your heart is still desiring the things of this world more than heavenly things, the pull of earthly pleasures will be very strong. This will be part of your "continued struggle" that you have not addressed. Ask yourself, "What are the specific ways in which earthly pleasures pull me back into the cesspool of sensuality?" If your heart is desiring heavenly things, God is enough for you. You find in Him a treasure and joy that the earthly life cannot fill.

Let me illustrate. If a poison is attacking the body's system, a doctor will seek to find the source. If the source is a part of the body that has become contaminated, a surgeon might have to cut it off in order to remove its influence on the rest of the body. How determined are you to not allow pornographic desires and images to control you?

It is amazing how we make excuses for our continued sensual input. We do not cut it off. We are truly blind to our problem. We are too

How serious are you? Are you really burdened that sensuality hold you in its chains? Write out your thoughts.

_____

_____

_____

_____

_____

_____

_____

Confess your weaknesses. Acknowledge your tendency to be easy on self.

Small groups: The Bible says that we are to confess our faults to one another. The honesty and transparency required improve the probability that you will change. If you are easy on yourself, others in your small group will lovingly and graciously be tough when you need it.

_____

_____

_____

_____

_____

_____

_____

_____

easy on ourselves. Jesus said that we must deny self (Matt. 16:24). Paul said that we must die to self (Rom. 6:7). In these verses Paul says we must amputate these affections and lusts. To do so, we must cut off whatever keeps fueling our lusts and infecting our souls.

Note
1 **Avis Christiansen.** Copyright 1961 Singspiration Music. Benson Music Group.

Day 5. Amputate! (2)

Daily Meditation Themes

- *Goodness and Greatness of God:* "For thus says the One who is high and lifted up, who inhabits eternity, whose name is Holy: 'I dwell in the high and holy place, and also with him who is of a contrite and lowly spirit, to revive the spirit of the lowly, and to revive the heart of the contrite'" (Isa. 57:15).

Song: "The Unveiled Christ"

Once our blessed Christ of beauty
Was veiled off from human view;
But through suffering, death, and sorrow
He has rent the veil in two.

O behold the Man of Sorrows,
O behold Him in plain view;
Lo! He is the mighty conqueror,
Since He rent the veil in two.
Lo! He is the mighty conqueror,
Since He rent the veil in two.

Throughout time and endless ages,
Heights and depths of love so true,
He alone shall be the giver,
Since He rent the veil in two.[1]

Meditation

You must remove the influences that do not pass the Philippians 4:8 test. Cut off—perform a radical amputation of—that which leads you into sensual life choices, thinking, and desires. Putting sinful ways to death in practice reminds us that Christ has done this with the power of sin and that before God He has justified us and made us righteous. These truths should be strong motivations for radical change.

How do you see God now? Does this kind of God motivate you to cut off fleshly and sensual habits?

Ask God for help!

93

Change happens in real life and real time. So make up your mind how this will work for you. What are you going to do?

_____

_____

_____

_____

_____

_____

_____

_____

_____

_____

_____

_____

_____

_____

Ask God for help!

_____

_____

_____

_____

_____

_____

_____

_____

_____

_____

_____

_____

_____

_____

- You must set up life patterns that will help you avoid lust.
- You must not allow others to pull you down or tell you that the changes you are making are too radical. *Holiness is radical to most people.* They will not understand why you cannot do what they do or why you will not watch what they watch. They cannot comprehend living life without the Internet or TV. In fact, several times I have watched the Youtube video about cutting out all online connection for a time. Focus on people and God, not all the stuff created by the online community. Try it.
- You must make a plan that helps you avoid all unhelpful influences that you can choose to avoid. God promises not to tempt you above what you are able to bear. Until you have established a pattern of victory over the lure of lust, you cannot afford to do what others may have freedom to do. And some things are just not worth the risk of losing the purity of your mind.
- In its place (you are dead, Paul says), set your mind on God! That is the purpose of our Daily Meditation Themes. Think on these things through the day.

Note
1 Noah B. Herrell, 1916.

Day 6. Review of the First Three Weeks

Daily Meditation Themes

- *Goodness of God:* "Lord, you have been our dwelling place in all generations" (Ps. 90:1).
- *Greatness of God:* "Blessed be the name of God forever and ever, to whom belong wisdom and might. He changes times and seasons; he removes kings and sets up kings; he gives wisdom to the wise and knowledge to those who have understanding; he reveals deep and hidden things; he knows what is in the darkness, and the light dwells with him" (Dan. 2:20–22).

Song: "I Will Glory in My Redeemer"

I will glory in my Redeemer
Whose priceless blood has ransomed me
Mine was the sin that drove the bitter nails
And hung Him on that judgment tree
I will glory in my Redeemer
Who crushed the power of sin and death
My only Savior before the Holy Judge
The Lamb who is my righteousness
The Lamb who is my righteousness

I will glory in my Redeemer
My life He bought, my love He owns
I have no longings for another
I'm satisfied in Him alone
I will glory in my Redeemer
His faithfulness my standing place
Though foes are mighty and rush upon me
My feet are firm, held by His grace
My feet are firm, held by His grace

I will glory in my Redeemer
Who carries me on eagles' wings
He crowns my life with loving kindness

What kind of attribute is everlasting? How does it help you in your struggle for a pure mind?

_____
_____
_____
_____
_____
_____
_____
_____
_____
_____
_____
_____
_____

What exactly do you think it means to give glory to the One who died for you?

_____
_____
_____
_____
_____
_____
_____
_____
_____
_____
_____
_____
_____
_____

Encourage yourself in God:

_____

_____

_____

_____

_____

_____

_____

_____

Write out your personal journey so far.

_____

_____

_____

_____

_____

_____

_____

_____

Small groups: Share what God has done for you so far. As often as possible, point to the evidence of God's grace at work. Rejoice with those who rejoice.

_____

_____

_____

_____

_____

_____

_____

_____

His triumph song I'll ever sing
I will glory in my Redeemer
Who waits for me at gates of gold
And when He calls me it will be paradise
His face forever to behold
His face forever to behold[1]

Meditation

Take time to enjoy the progress God has worked in you already. Remind yourself of the powerful truths that are now beginning to take root in your heart. You have not only learned that the battle you face is something that many others face as well, but you have also begun to understand the ways and means that Satan uses to get at your inner being to lead you into temptation. You know now that God has given you the means to defeat the world, the flesh, and the devil. You have the truths of Romans 6–8 as an anchor in your daily life. You can determine to win, and plan to win, the daily battle for your heart, its thinking and desires. Your pattern of daily meditation on God's nature and goodness should begin to turn your desires away from the cheapness of pleasing self and indulging in sensuality to ultimate satisfaction in Christ and in your relationship with Him.

Take time now to read Romans 8:28–39 and give thanks to God for the glorious truth that nothing can change God's love for you. Remind yourself of the goal—becoming like Christ (v. 29)—and thank God for the transformation taking place in your heart and life. Read Hebrews 12:5–11 and see how even God's chastening hand is evidence of God's love toward us. Don't miss this wonderful truth. If you could live on in your pornography and not "get caught" or have your sin exposed, would that matter to God? The answer is, Yes. First, it matters because of God's glory and His name. Second, it matters because He loves you enough to not let you remain in your sin. So God exposes your sin so that you can deal with it. God's love reveals itself in sin-confronting ways.

You know that you must put away the patterns of sin that have troubled you. You are beginning to see sin's allure before you even go down the path. This is a good change. Remember that before, you were blind to sin's power over you. Your conscience did not even trouble you regarding your choices in sensual living and pleasure. Now you are sensitized rather than desensitized. You have begun to enjoy your walk with God and are starting to know what it is like to hate sin and love God with all your heart and soul and mind.

Ezekiel 8 contains a fascinating description of the idolatry that was present in Israel during Ezekiel's time. Notice that this idolatry was such that the glory of God (v. 4) was departing from Israel (9:3). God describes their activities as abominations—"great abominations" (v. 6). The word "abominations" is reserved for what God detests most in His people. Can you see how your hidden idolatry is equally vile and detestable to God?

The people of Israel were worshipping in the dark, supposedly hiding their activities, their "vile abominations" (v. 9). One of these abominations, the "image of jealousy," was out in the open (v. 3), but much of what the elders—the supposed leadership of the people—were doing (worshipping beasts, creeping things, the sun, and probably sensual pictures) was in private, hidden.

What a potent example of what it is like for people to have their hearts filled with things that God sees as wicked, vile abominations! We behave similarly when we allow our sensual lusts to be hidden in the darkness of our hearts, our closets, behind our closed office doors, and in secret with our computers, our cell phones,

Your thoughts on Ezekiel 8:

_____

_____

_____

_____

_____

_____

_____

_____

_____

_____

_____

_____

_____

Describe how God responds to idolatry.

_____

_____

_____

_____

_____

_____

_____

_____

_____

_____

_____

_____

_____

_____

and our video watching in our homes late at night. We think that God does not notice or care (Ez. 8:12).

How can we "hide" from God? We are like Adam and Eve in the Garden. We really think that we can somehow get away with this. What blindness sin brings! This blindness is described in Hebrews 3:13 as the "deceitfulness of sin." This verse says that we need daily to exhort one another in ways that help us recognize our deceitful hearts.

Note

1 Music and words by **Steve & Vikki Cook** © 2000 Sovereign Grace Worship (ASCAP). www. SovereignGraceMusic.org. Used with permission.

Day 7. Focus on the Cross

This week we need to remind ourselves that before Christ went to the cross, He had already faced the incredible pain of scourging. The Gospels report this event with just a sentence or two: "Then Pilate took Jesus and flogged him" (John 19:1). A short sentence like this does not do justice to such an excruciating event.

Isaiah 52–53 perhaps gives us a brief look at this painful event as well. The Messiah is already "marred" (52:14) and He has lost the beauty of His person. He is bruised and has "wounds" on His body on our behalf (53:5). Scourging rips flesh and leaves the sufferer in terrible pain.

Behold, my servant shall act wisely;
    and he shall be high and lifted up,
    and shall be exalted.
As many were astonished at you—
    his appearance was so marred, beyond
    human semblance,
and his form beyond that of the children of
    mankind …
he had no form or majesty that we should look
    at him,
    and no beauty that we should desire him …
yet we esteemed him stricken,
    smitten by God, and afflicted.
But he was pierced for our transgressions;
    he was crushed for our iniquities …
Yet it was the will of the LORD to crush him.
                    (Isa. 52:13–14; 53:2, 4–5, 10)

When they put the crown of thorns on his head and drive it into his skull, it only adds to the pain he is already experiencing. Then they put a cloak around him to continue the masquerade of royalty and play games with

Your thoughts:

_____

_____

_____

_____

_____

_____

_____

_____

_____

_____

_____

_____

Small groups: We are used to watching a lot of violence on TV, even in the news, and especially in movies. Discuss how we become desensitized to violence in such a way that the cross does little to move us.

_____

_____

_____

_____

_____

_____

_____

_____

_____

Thoughts on God:

_____
_____
_____
_____
_____
_____
_____
_____
_____
_____
_____
_____
_____
_____

Thoughts on the cross:

_____
_____
_____
_____
_____
_____
_____
_____
_____
_____
_____
_____
_____
_____

Him. Through this ordeal, the blood is soaking the robe, which they will pull from his back to further amplify the pain he is experiencing. There is no way we can begin to comprehend the agonizing pain that He experienced on our behalf.

The object of the scourging was to weaken victims to a state of collapse and bring them as near to death as possible without actually killing them. Many did not survive this punishment and it was given the name "half death." The extent of loss of blood may well have determined how long the victim would survive on the cross.

Daily Meditation Theme

- *Greatness of God:* "How great are his signs, how mighty his wonders! His kingdom is an everlasting kingdom, and his dominion endures from generation to generation ... I blessed the Most High, and praised and honored him who lives forever ... all the inhabitants of the earth are accounted as nothing, and he does according to his will among the host of heaven and among the inhabitants of the earth; and none can stay his hand or say to him, 'What have you done?' ... I ... praise and extol and honor the King of heaven, for all his works are right and his ways are just" (Dan. 4:3, 34–35, 37).

Song: "When I Survey the Wondrous Cross"

When I survey the wondrous cross
On which the Prince of Glory died,
My richest gain I count but loss,
And pour contempt on all my pride.

Forbid it, Lord, that I should boast,
Save in the death of Christ my God!

All the vain things that charm me most,
I sacrifice them to His blood.

See, from His head, His hands, His feet,
Sorrow and love flow mingled down;
Did e'er such love and sorrow meet,
Or thorns compose so rich a crown?

Were the whole realm of nature mine,
That were a present far too small;
Love so amazing, so divine,
Demands my soul, my life, my all.[1]

Note

1 Isaac Watts, 1707.

Week 4.
Rebuild the Mind

When we understand Week 1's material on the heart, we see that we have a great need in this battle for the body and mind: to make sure that our hearts are thinking right thoughts about God, ourselves, sin, and the world around us. We must constantly be aware how the world and its media attack God, soften sin, and focus on looking good on the outside. If we are not adjusting our thinking to reflect biblical principles, we are simply not thinking biblically. This wrong thinking will always lead to wrong desires and wrong choices. They are inextricably joined together within our hearts.

In Week 3 we emphasized the negative activity that must take place in seeking a pure life. We must put off the old nature that is corrupt. We must deny self. We must flee the lusts that plague foolish people. But if our lives are based on putting off sinful desires and we never get to the positive, we will be doomed to failure. Without a "putting on" of the new nature and the developing of a renewed mind we cannot expect purity to become a life pattern.

Unfortunately, in many Bible-preaching churches, schools, and Christian homes, "putting off" is the only emphasis given. The lines of sin are drawn. The boxes of good and bad are constructed. The fences are marked to set certain things as off-limits. But little is done to feed the heart and develop desires for God. So when the chains of protection start to break and the boundaries of sin are broken, parents, pastors, and leaders cannot understand how their children, students, and co-workers could give in to pornography, extramarital sex, and other immoral acts. Did they not warn against such lasciviousness (the very word sounds wicked to the conservative Christian ear)? How could they have gone wrong? By only emphasizing what *not* to do. Therefore, we must also emphasize the need to develop hearts that passionately pursue God. This is why the Daily Meditation Themes are essential in this book. Furthermore, small groups are also a biblical and essential factor in helping one another in this process. We can make sure that we are not just trying to "say no," but that we are also meditating on and enjoying the wonder of God.

Day 1. View of God (1):
The Attributes of God

Daily Meditation Themes

- *Goodness of God:* "Satisfy us in the morning with your steadfast love, that we may rejoice and be glad all our days" (Ps. 90:14). "Praise the LORD! For it is good to sing praises to our God; for it is pleasant, and a song of praise is fitting ... Great is our Lord, and abundant in power; his understanding is beyond measure ... Sing to the LORD with thanksgiving; make melody to our God on the lyre!" (Ps. 147:1, 5, 7).

- *Greatness of God:* "'Therefore thus will I do to you, O Israel; because I will do this to you, prepare to meet your God, O Israel!' For behold, he who forms the mountains and creates the wind, and declares to man what is his thought, who makes the morning darkness, and treads on the heights of the earth—the LORD, the God of hosts, is his name!" (Amos 4:12–13).

Song: "In Christ Alone"

In Christ alone my hope is found;
He is my light, my strength, my song;
This cornerstone, this solid ground,
Firm through the fiercest drought and storm.
What heights of love, what depths of peace,
When fears are stilled, when strivings cease!
My comforter, my all in all—
Here in the love of Christ I stand.

In Christ alone, Who took on flesh,
Fullness of God in helpless babe!
This gift of love and righteousness,

Thoughts on God:

The character of God: He is holy and demands a holy people. Do you believe that? Do you doubt that God is really that holy and pure?

_____

_____

_____

_____

_____

God is good. Do you think He has done right by you? Do you think you got left out? Do you doubt that God gives you all you need or all that is good? Do you doubt God's goodness?

_____

_____

_____

_____

_____

God is in control. Do you believe this, or do you think that God lets things happen that hurt you and so now you deserve to get back at God? Is your anger or bitterness at God the seed bed for immoral thoughts?

_____

_____

_____

_____

_____

Small groups: Take the topics above and be honest about where you are in your practical theology.

Scorned by the ones He came to save.
Till on that cross as Jesus died,
The wrath of God was satisfied;
For ev'ry sin on Him was laid—
Here in the death of Christ I live.

No guilt in life, no fear in death—
This is the pow'r of Christ in me;
From life's first cry to final breath,
Jesus commands my destiny.
No pow'r of hell, no scheme of man,
Can ever pluck me from His hand;
Till He returns or calls me home—
Here in the pow'r of Christ I'll stand.[1]

Meditation

One of the fundamental changes that must take place in our hearts in order for there to be a renewal of purity in our lives is in the way we view God. If our view of God is poor, we will definitely slip back into our old patterns of sin. The only reason we will view our inner being as naturally wicked is if we have the right view of God. When we view God as holy, glorious, and all-knowing, we will react to these incredible truths as their reality sinks in to our hearts. We will be moved to be more like Him and less like the world. But when we think that God ignores sin, is removed from the hard reality of daily life, and does not care much how we live, we will live more like the world.

- Some find it hard to believe that God really does love us or that He really is in control of things; we can doubt the Bible truth that gives us hope and enables us to see the stranglehold of sin on our lives.
- We may have experienced things that have caused us to disbelieve the truth about God's goodness and righteousness. We see Him as hard, life as hard, and God as unforgiving.

- We lose sight of the cross and His sacrifice for us. The result is that we slip into sin patterns that appease our flesh.
- We feel we deserve some worldly pleasure, considering the tough life situations we have been given. We begin to see God as far removed from our struggles, and we have no real concept of Christ's being a High Priest who understands our passions, temptations, and the pull of our hearts toward the world.

If this is how you feel, spend some time comparing how you live and look at life with how you view God. Look at the chart on the next two pages[2] to see the ways in which your mind might have been infiltrated with a poor view of God. Notice how the attributes (characteristics) of God directly apply to your battle for a pure mind and pure body. Here is an example:

- *God knows all things.* But does God know what I am thinking? Does it really matter anyway? If God knows, why doesn't He stop me? What does God know about the future? Will He interfere, or will He allow me to make my own choices? Is God so busy handling events in the rest of the world that my little situation really does not matter much?
- *God is all-powerful.* If God is this powerful, why does He allow bad things to happen to me? I don't feel as if He really cares. I have bitterness in my heart. Why? God knows and sees the bad things in my life and He has not prevented them. I feel I deserve to have some fun and some of the pleasure that is out there in the world.

Notes

1 Keith Getty and Stuart Townend. Copyright 2001 Thankyou Music. EMI Christian Music Publishing.

2 Material in the chart is taken from a study produced by the staff at The Wilds Christian Association, Taylors, SC, and is used with permission.

GOD IS ...	DEFINED	EXPLAINED	DEMONSTRATED
All-knowing	God fully knows all things–past, present, and future.	Prov. 15:3 Matt. 10:30	Dan. 2
All-powerful	God is free and able to do whatever He wants.	Jer. 32:17 Eph. 3:20	Gen. 18:9–15
All-present	God is present everywhere at all times.	1 Kings 8:27 Jer. 23:23–24	Jonah 1–2
Faithful	God is reliable. God will always do what He has said and fulfill what He has promised.	Num. 23:19 Deut. 7:9 2 Tim. 2:13	Rom. 4:13–25
Good	God is the ultimate standard of good, and all that He does is worthy of approval.	Ps. 34:8 Luke 18:19	Gen. 1
Gracious	God is kind toward those who do not deserve it.	Eph. 2:7–9 Titus 2:11	Acts 9:1–22
Holy	God is absolutely pure. He is separate from all that is unclean and evil.	1 John 1:5 Ps. 99:9	Exod. 19:9–25

Love	God eternally gives of Himself for the good of others.	1 John 4:7–8 John 3:16 Rom. 5:8	John 19:1–37
Merciful/Patient	God is slow to anger, and because of Christ does not give us the punishment that we deserve.	Ps. 103:8 Isa. 55:7	John 8:3–11
Righteous/Just	God is the ultimate standard of what is right. He will always punish the wicked and reward the righteous, without favoritism.	Ps. 19:9 Acts 17:31	Rev. 19
Sovereign/In Control	God rules over His creation. He actively guides all events to fulfill His purpose.	Isa. 46:9–10 Prov. 21:1	Gen. 37:18–36; 50:19–21
Sufficient	God is more than enough. He alone satisfies.	Heb. 13:5 2 Cor. 3:5	Eccles. 2:1–11; 12:13–14
Supreme	God is first, above all, chief, supreme.	Col. 1:16–17 1 Cor. 8:6	Dan. 4

Day 2. View of God (2)

God is all-knowing. Do you think He sees us when we are involved in our sensuality? What do you really think?

E.g. I think God does not really spend time watching me. He does not really care if I look at a little immodesty or enjoy a little extramarital sex.

God is just. He will do what is right. He will judge sin. Do you really think you will get away with your sin?

God is longsuffering. He gives you much time to repent. How?

Daily Meditation Themes

- *Goodness of God:* "Who is to condemn? Christ Jesus is the one who died—more than that, who was raised—who is at the right hand of God, who indeed is interceding for us" (Rom. 8:34).
- *Greatness of God:* "Let your work be shown to your servants, and your glorious power to their children" (Ps. 90:16). "The LORD is high above all nations, and his glory above the heavens! Who is like the LORD our God, who is seated on high …?" (113:4–5).

Song: "Before the Throne of God Above"

Before the throne of God above
I have a strong and perfect plea.
A great High Priest whose name is Love,
Who ever lives and pleads for me.
My name is graven on His hands,
My name is written on His heart.
I know that while in Heaven He stands
No tongue can bid me thence depart.

When Satan tempts me to despair
And tells me of the guilt within,
Upward I look and see Him there,
Who made an end of all my sin.
Because the sinless Savior died
My sinful soul is counted free.
For God the Just is satisfied,
To look on Him and pardon me.

Behold Him there, the risen Lamb,
My perfect spotless righteousness,
The great unchangeable I AM,
The King of glory and of grace,
One in Himself I cannot die.
My soul is purchased by His blood,

My life is hid with Christ on high,
With Christ my Savior and my God![1]

Meditation

Let's look briefly at God's goodness and greatness. You can come back to this later for further encouragement in your journey toward godliness. Knowing a good and great God in all His "fullness" as best we humanly can certainly enlarges our souls. It cannot help but move us away from a temporal and sensual world toward the eternal and holy God.

THE GREATNESS OF GOD

God is Spirit. Each of us, on the other hand, has a spirit. We are confined to our bodies, while God is infinite and not limited to any geographical location. He operates (exists and works) outside the material creation. He can be anywhere and everywhere He wants to be. He is not limited to any space anywhere. He is outside of our material, created realm. That is part of what makes Him God and not like man. Since God brought all of space, time, and matter into being, He simply is (His name Jehovah means "I AM"). This means that He can be somewhere specific and everywhere at the same time. He is transcendent. He is above our way of expressing life and being. In Psalm 139 the psalmist says that there is no place in the universe that is inaccessible to God. We can't hide from Him. Therefore we should never question whether God is here or not. His presence does not depend on how life is going for us or how well we are doing in the battle against temptation. We may not "feel that God is here," but we must believe it to be true and act accordingly. Nor is God restricted by time. He is Alpha and Omega, the beginning and the end. He does not change, grow, or develop. He needs no more knowledge or input. No one teaches Him. He never grows old. He is

Specific, personal application:

_____
_____
_____
_____
_____
_____
_____
_____
_____

Small groups: Discuss which attributes of God you find most difficult to accept or believe. Why?

_____
_____
_____
_____
_____
_____
_____

In what specific ways will you live differently in the light of these attributes?

_____
_____
_____
_____
_____
_____

Small groups: Discuss the difficulty of prayer. Prayer is talking to someone who is there but whom we can't see. God is Spirit. But when we praise Him for His goodness and greatness, we must sense in our inner being the reality of the conversation.

---

beyond time's effects and above its limits. He is unlimited in every realm of knowledge. He knows all contingencies and possibilities. He is without limit in His power. If He wants to work in nature He can do anything, whether using supernatural or natural phenomena. The miraculous for God is just normal. And yet, in exercising His power, He never contradicts any other part of His character. God is amazing. Part of what makes Him amazing is that although He is transcendent, God is also immanent (near). He is involved in our lives.

THE GOODNESS OF GOD

God is trustworthy in handling His greatness because He is good. If God were not good, He might blow us out of existence with His power. But He does not. His mercy and love, His patience and longsuffering nature assure us that God will always exercise all His unlimited abilities in a way that is consistent with His being just and holy—morally good. God will always have pure thoughts, righteous motives, and just desires. His perfection is the basis of His commands for us to live pure lives. God always acts in conformity to this standard. His integrity demands that He act as He demands of us. He is not outside of His law; He mirrors His law. He is true. God cannot lie. He must always and invariably communicate and relate to us through truth. We can count on God's truthfulness. There is no facade with God. We don't have to wonder what we will find if we really get to know Him. How can we express the fact that God loves us? He defined His love for us on the cross. The cross is His love exegeted in full. We can know that God is concerned about us because of Calvary. He cares for the birds (Matt. 6:26), so we can know He cares about us. He loves us for no other reason than that He chose to shower upon us His love. This is a great and generous God:

great in His generosity to undeserving you and me. We do not deserve anything; our lives themselves are founded on mercy. We gain all in Him and so life is also filled with grace. This is unfathomable.

We should not move out of this study too quickly because so much of what we do in life comes from this theological basis. In fact, it is not overstating the case to say that our lives are simply a reflection of what we think and believe about God. Every kind of sin reflects this reality, for we do what we do because of what we believe about God and because of the desires in our hearts. The desires of our hearts change when what we think about God changes. So these inner-being (heart) battles are all connected to what we really, truly, think about God. Today, spend time being honest about what your sensual struggles and your thought-life reveal about your view of God.

Take time working through the sidebars and look back at yesterday's table of the characteristics of God. Decide which aspects of this study you doubt or deny by your continued pursuit of sensual pleasure and gratification. Make sure you are thorough, because this is part of what you must change in your heart's thinking and desiring.

Note

1 Words by **Charitie Lees Bancroft.** Music and alternate words by **Vikki Cook.** © 1997 Sovereign Grace Worship (ASCAP). www.SovereignGraceMusic. org. Used with permission.

Small groups: Take time to share in the group some of God's goodness to you personally. Public praise of God by those who know God is a nail in the coffin of sensuality and pleasing self.

Day 3. Made in God's Image (1)

God thoughts:

_____
_____
_____
_____
_____
_____
_____
_____
_____
_____
_____
_____
_____

Write a short meditation on God and His love:

_____
_____
_____
_____
_____
_____
_____
_____
_____
_____
_____
_____
_____
_____
_____
_____

Daily Meditation Themes

- _Goodness of God:_ "Let the favor [or beauty] of the Lord our God be upon us and establish the work of our hands upon us" (Ps. 90:17). "Be exalted, O God, above the heavens! Let your glory be over all the earth!" (108:5).
- _Greatness of God:_ "Therefore you are great, O LORD God. For there is none like you … according to all that we have heard with our ears. And who is like your people Israel, the one nation on earth whom God went to redeem to be his people, making himself a name and doing for them great and awesome things …? And your name will be magnified forever, saying, 'The LORD of hosts is God over Israel'" (2 Sam. 7:22–23, 26).

Song: "How Deep the Father's Love for Us"

How deep the Father's love for us,
How vast beyond all measure
That He should give His only Son
To make a wretch His treasure.
How great the pain of searing loss,
The Father turns His face away.
As wounds which mar the chosen One,
Bring many sons to glory.

Behold the Man upon a cross,
My sin upon His shoulders
Ashamed I hear my mocking voice,
Call out among the scoffers
It was my sin that left Him there
Until it was accomplished
His dying breath has brought me life
I know that it is finished.

I will not boast in anything

No gifts, no power, no wisdom
But I will boast in Jesus Christ
His death and resurrection
Why should I gain from His reward?
I cannot give an answer
But this I know with all my heart
His wounds have paid my ransom.[1]

Meditation

Once we have adjusted our thinking about God to conform to the biblical pattern, we must also adjust our thinking about ourselves. Part of the problem that drives sensual thinking comes out of our view of men and women. We must see them as made "in the image of God" (Gen. 1:27). This is totally different from the cultural model we find around us.

Being made in the image of God indicates what is unique about man compared with the rest of creation. This idea of *image* is at the heart of anthropology and sanctification. Man is a being whose existence is a reflection of God in some way. The fact that we are humankind rather than animal "kind" includes the fact that we bear the image of God.

The basic thought behind the word "image" (*eikonos*, Rom. 8:29) is that of *likeness*; we are like God in some aspects. If we were exactly like him, we would be God, but instead man was created with similarities to God. This likeness is a reflection of God. It is like the image we see when we look in a mirror. Although all creation reveals God in some way, this is especially the case with man. What an honor to reveal God to the world around us! We can reveal God's love, kindness, and goodness. A tree reflects a Creator, but a man or woman reflects God's moral character.

Theologians disagree about how much of God's image is reflected in man. The core of this likeness is found in man's personality and attributes. It is the inner being that

Define the concept of "image" in your own words.

Can you take time to thank God for this likeness of God in you?

Small groups: Does everyone in your group "get it" regarding "image bearing"? Write out your own thoughts about this truth of imaging God.

Dave's testimony: *This truth has revolutionized my approach to life in many ways. But I think most of all it has helped me understand how I am to look at other people. I now tend to see them much less as those I can use for my own ends, instead recognizing in them the purpose and image of God.*

Make a list of things that have become items in *your* idolatry closet—those things you bring out to worship when no one else is around (except for God—we already know that we treat Him as if He is not really there).

_____
_____
_____
_____
_____

Small groups: What has been wrong with your view of sex and men and women? How would you put into words your view of the opposite gender? Discuss what our culture tends to portray about men and women and how they should relate to one another.

_____
_____
_____
_____
_____
_____

differentiates us most from the rest of creation. Yet we can also see that the human body is part of what God created "in his image," and we know that the body will be resurrected in its perfect form to enjoy fellowship with God.

To further understand the word "image" we must think through its meaning with regard to function. We can consider what kind of man God made, but we must also understand what man does. Structurally, man was made in such a way that "the entire endowment of gifts and capacities … enable man to function as he should in his various relationships and callings."[2] Some of the types of characteristics man exhibits are easily traceable to God's nature:

- Intellectual: we have the ability to study and know truth
- Rational: we reflect the fact that God is a reasoning being
- Morality: we can reflect the moral knowledge of what is right and wrong
- Worship: we can speak and sing for God and about God
- Volition: we can have purpose in life

We must also reflect on what God says about how we are to become more like Him:

- "… put on the new self, which is being renewed in knowledge after the image of its creator" (Col. 3:10)
- "… put on the new self, created after the likeness of God in true righteousness and holiness" (Eph. 4:24)

These verses point to the way men and women function in harmony with God's will for them. The fall of man into sin and rebellion against God has damaged the way we reflect God. We reflect Him in an imperfect way. "What makes sin so serious is precisely the fact that man is now using God-given and God-imaging powers and gifts to do things that are an affront to his Maker."[3] Man is still made in the image of God even though he is depraved and sinful by choice and nature. He is still different from the other parts of creation: all the characteristics of man that make him unique and God-directed are still there. Yet they are affected by the Fall. The more affected man is by the Fall, the less he seems to reflect God's image. However, we must pursue God's image until we die.

Notes

1 **Stuart Townend,** 1995. Thankyou Music. EMI Christian Music Publishing.

2 **Anthony Hoekema,** *Created in God's Image* (Grand Rapids, MI: Eerdmans, 1986), 70–71.

3 Ibid., 72.

Day 4. Made in God's Image (2)

God thoughts:

_____
_____
_____
_____
_____
_____
_____
_____
_____
_____
_____
_____
_____
_____
_____
_____

What is the songwriter saying?

_____
_____
_____
_____
_____
_____
_____
_____
_____
_____
_____
_____

Daily Meditation Themes

- *Goodness of God:* "Glory in his holy name; let the hearts of those who seek the LORD rejoice! Seek the LORD and his strength; seek his presence continually!" (Ps. 105:3–4). "For you know the grace of our Lord Jesus Christ, that though he was rich, yet for your sakes he became poor, so that you by his poverty might become rich" (2 Cor. 8:9).
- *Greatness of God:* in 1 Kings 17, see how God hides Elijah, God uses ravens to feed Elijah, and God provides an endless supply of oil for the widow and raises her son from the dead.

Song: "Jesus, the Very Thought of Thee"

Jesus, the very thought of Thee
With sweetness fills my breast;
But sweeter far Thy face to see,
And in Thy presence rest.

Nor voice can sing, nor heart can frame,
Nor can the mem'ry find
A sweeter sound than Thy blest name,
O Savior of mankind!

O Hope of every contrite heart,
O Joy of all the meek,
To those who fall, how kind Thou art!
How good to those who seek!

But what to those who find? Ah, this
Nor tongue nor pen can show;
The love of Jesus, what it is
None but His loved ones know.

Jesus, our only Joy be Thou,
As Thou our Prize wilt be;

Jesus, be Thou our Glory now,
And through eternity.[1]

Meditation

The truth about sin and man's ability to mirror God also helps us to see how man works his way by grace back toward pleasing God again once he has a new nature. The abilities and gifts are already present in man to be used for God's glory and to fulfill His original plan. The renewing of the image of God in man is the sanctification process. Man's function is the primary way he reflects his God. Man's structure is secondary.

Now, let's apply this truth of God's image in man to the issue of moral purity. Idolatry has been the chief result of man's fall. In worshiping self, we put how we feel and what we want and desire above that which God wants of us. In worshiping others, we put other people's acceptance of us or control over us above the glory of God.[2] Our thinking is skewed by our fallen natures. Our hearts drive us away from godliness and God-imaging. But there are several steps we can take back in the right direction. We must depend on God's grace and power to change our hearts. We can infuse our hearts with God's Word so that we start thinking right thoughts once again about God and about ourselves. Right thinking will produce right desires.

If you are taken up with pornography and/or sensual and sinful physical relationships with others, it is necessary to renew the image of God within you. Several facets of your life must change in order for you to image God correctly and also view others as image-bearers.

- You must begin to see all of life, including sex, as God-given and beautiful.
- You must not live according to your fallen feelings and desires.

Men: write in your own words what God says about women.

_____

_____

_____

_____

_____

_____

_____

Small groups: What should our focus be when we look at someone of the opposite sex?

_____

_____

_____

_____

_____

What should a woman say about herself before God?

_____

_____

_____

_____

_____

_____

_____

_____

_____

Explain what God says through Genesis 1 and creation about women's ability to be like God.

_____
_____
_____
_____
_____
_____
_____
_____
_____
_____

What should a woman be focused on when she sees a man or is in a relationship with a man?

_____
_____
_____
_____
_____
_____

What do you think a woman's greatest temptation is with a man?

_____
_____
_____
_____
_____
_____
_____
_____

- You must recognize the need for self-control through the Spirit.
- You must allow God's grace and love to help you love others properly.
- You must see other people clearly as image-bearers who are God's property.
- You must recognize the commandment to love and care for others before yourself.

Now let's apply the principle of image-bearing to men's attitude to women (tomorrow we will look at women's attitude to men). The ultimate reason God created woman was to be a help-meet for Adam. Thus, a wife is to help her husband reflect, image, and demonstrate the character of God in his life. A woman who is single is created first to fulfill her responsibility to her God.

The characteristics listed below are found in all women:

- *Intellectual:* Women have the ability to study and know truth. Men should focus on helping women know God through His Word and appraising their struggles with the effects of the Fall on their lives.
- *Rational:* Women reflect the fact that God is a reasoning being; they can think like Him in logical and specific ways that help both men and women understand creation and the issues of life. Men are to help them think through the effects of all revelation on our world.
- *Moral:* Women can reflect the moral purity of God in the way they treat their bodies for God's glory. They are part of God's creation. They belong to Him. They know right from wrong.
- *Worshipful:* Women have the ability to speak and sing for God and about God.
- *Volitional:* Women can choose between right and wrong. They can have purpose in life for God and not just for men. Men must see women as image-bearers of God. They

must see that every woman is made in God's image, regardless of how pure or impure she is in her lifestyle. They need to stop looking at women as bodies made for their eyes and for their sensual desires to abuse. A man's mindset must change so that he thinks about a woman's heart and her need to glorify God and fulfill His purposes through her life, especially if that means she needs salvation. Men, see the reflection of God when you look at a woman's face.

Notes

1 Attrib. **Bernard of Clairvaux,** 12th century; transl. **Edward Caswall.**

2 For those dealing with same-sex struggles, this idolatry is a huge factor. Fear of man and worshiping man's acceptance drives the lust for same-sex relationships, even though they are contrary to God's plan. The nature of this study, however, does not allow me to deal with "same-sex attraction." Having counseled men who struggle with this, I realize there are a number of additional steps of maturity and change that need to take place *before* they can tackle this present study on purity of life. Their heart idols and their thoughts about themselves and about others must change.

Day 5. Made in God's Image (3)

God thoughts:

_____
_____
_____
_____
_____
_____
_____
_____
_____
_____
_____
_____
_____
_____

Small groups: Consider God's attributes. What does *mercy* contribute to God's character and to our lives?

_____
_____
_____
_____
_____
_____
_____
_____
_____
_____
_____
_____
_____

Daily Meditation Themes

- *Goodness of God:* "Oh come, let us sing to the LORD; let us make a joyful noise to the rock of our salvation!" (Ps. 95:1).
- *Greatness of God:* "'O LORD, the God of Israel, enthroned above the cherubim, you are the God, you alone, of all the kingdoms of the earth; you have made heaven and earth. Incline your ear, O LORD, and hear; open your eyes, O LORD, and see; and hear the words of Sennacherib, which he has sent to mock the living God.' ... 'Whom have you mocked and reviled? Against whom have you raised your voice and lifted your eyes to the heights? Against the Holy One of Israel!'" (2 Kings 19:15–16, 22)

Song: "Mercies Anew"

Every morning that breaks there are mercies anew.
Every breath that I take is your faithfulness proved,
And at the end of each day, when my labors are
    through,
I will sing of Your mercies anew.

When I've fallen and strayed there were
    mercies anew.
For you sought me in love and my heart you
    pursued.
In the face of my sin, Lord, You never withdrew.
So I sing of Your mercies anew.

And Your mercies they will never end;
For ten thousand years they'll remain.
And when this world's beauty has passed away,
Your mercies will be unchanged.

And when the storms swirl and rage,
    there are mercies anew.
In affliction and pain, You will carry me through.

And at the end of my days, when Your throne
  fills my view,
I will sing of Your mercies anew.
I will sing of Your mercies anew.[1]

Meditation

Today we'll apply this principle of image-bearing to women's attitude to men. Women can often feel insecure and seek men's approval. A woman who has grown up in a home where the father did not show love toward her and acceptance of her is especially vulnerable to this tendency. Such a home background does not mean she is destined to be a lust-driven individual, but it does make her vulnerable to this human tendency. Her old nature wants the approval of a man. Unless she finds this satisfaction in God, she will spend her early adult life looking for fulfillment and security in someone or something. She begins to find her security in a man's admiration and desire for her.

Eventually, she will be willing to exchange his desire for her body for her satisfaction of being wanted. Her lust is not for sex but to be loved and wanted. This is a sinful tendency in all of us. We turn from God to people for satisfaction. The world tells us that we have a need to be wanted and loved. Yet the Bible says we have a need *to love God and others, not to be loved.*[2] We have reversed God's order. We already love ourselves.

When a woman fantasizes about a man, she is looking and thinking about him for selfish purposes. If she has read romance novels, she may fantasize about meeting him in a moonlit, romantic setting where a very seductive and sensual scene takes place. She can imagine the kind of person who will come and want her.

This kind of woman is not focused on the man's inner person and his imaging of God. If she were, it would drive her to see how he was

Explain what you are seeing about the idolatry of a woman's heart.

_____

_____

_____

_____

_____

_____

_____

_____

_____

_____

_____

_____

What can a woman do in her God-focus to overcome early years of abuse? How does considering God's attributes help?

_____

_____

_____

_____

_____

_____

_____

_____

_____

_____

_____

_____

Small groups: Discuss how you would classify yourself: are you the abused or the abuser? Are you a "victim" of other people's attention, or a pursuer who wants the attention?

_____

_____

_____

_____

_____

_____

_____

How do you think you can find your security and identity in Christ?

_____

_____

_____

_____

_____

What do you think is God's purpose for your life?

_____

_____

_____

_____

_____

_____

_____

_____

_____

seeking God, getting to know God better, and pursuing God's glory in his life. However, since she wants his attention, approval, and desires for her body, she will use whatever means she can—those she has learned from watching other women attract men—to pursue him. She will watch men to see what they respond to and what they lust after. She will wear clothes that draw attention to her body. She will act in seductive ways to arouse his interest. She is not attracting a man to her God-like qualities. She is trying to get a man to like what he sees and lusts after (which he will enjoy until he decides to discard her and move on. You can see this happen in the story of Amnon in 2 Sam. 13).

It is evident that many women want to get men's attention. A woman may get a thrill by attracting men and dumping them, just so she knows she "has it" (the ability to attract and please men). She gets as much thrill in that as a man does in conquering a woman for his lust.

A woman who has been abused in her youth has added struggles in her mind and emotions that will drive her to seek a man's desire for her body. If she has never known a man who loves her for her inner being, she will not know that she can reflect God in this way. Since she feels used, she feels the need to prove her worth to a man. Yet the most necessary drive in her heart must be to restore God's beauty in her inner being. She should want God's glory to shine in her life. Otherwise, she will worship at the altar of man's approval and lust. She must stop lusting for acceptance. Instead, she must look for a godly man who does the following:

- Desires to know and study God's Word
- Understands the creation and the ways of God: that God as King is to be reverenced and worshiped
- Reflects God's holiness in his body and desires

- Sets his conscience in line with desires for purity
- Worships God in his heart and life

Notes

1 Music and words by **Mark Altrogge** and **Bob Kauflin** © 2002 Sovereign Grace Praise (BMI). www.SovereignGraceMusic.org. Used with permission.

2 Ed Welch's book (*When People Are Big and God Is Small* [Phillipsburg, NJ: P&R, 1997]) is an excellent help in this area of thinking.

Day 6. A Day of Meditation

Now do your own exercise in meditation on the glory and majesty of our great God.

_____
_____
_____
_____
_____
_____
_____
_____

How could you use this for a daily pattern of thinking on God?

_____
_____
_____
_____
_____
_____

Small groups: If you wanted to encourage someone else to do this activity, how would you describe the benefit you get from it?

_____
_____
_____
_____
_____
_____
_____
_____

Daily Meditation Themes

- *Goodness of God:* "He gives wisdom to the wise and knowledge to those who have understanding" (Dan. 2:21).
- *Greatness of God:* "Truly your God is God of gods and Lord of kings, and a revealer of mysteries" (Dan. 2:47).

Song: "O Great God"

O great God of highest heav'n
Occupy my lowly heart
Own it all and reign supreme
Conquer ever rebel pow'r
Let no vice or sin remain
That resists Your holy war
You have loved and purchased me
Make me Yours forevermore

I was blinded by my sin
Had no ears to hear Your voice
Did not know Your love within
Had no taste for heaven's joys
Then Your Spirit gave me life,
Opened up Your Word to me
Through the gospel of Your Son
Gave me endless hope and peace

Help me now to live a life
That's dependent on Your grace
Keep my heart and guard my soul
From the evils that I face
You are worthy to be praised
With my every thought and deed
O great God of highest heav'n
Glorify Your Name through me[1]

Meditation

By this point in your journey you will be beginning to appreciate the impact of meditating on something or someone so vast and good as God. Let me help you move forward and gain an even more powerful grasp of the power of this process of letting your mind and heart think on and enjoy God. We do not immediately sense the value of meditating on God, so it's important to reinforce this core activity.

When someone tells you that the Grand Canyon is impressive, you might nod and perhaps say, "Yes." But your agreement might be based purely on mental assent; it might not be emotionally grounded in your own experience of this natural phenomenon. In order for you to be impacted by the reality of the Canyon, you must actually see it. So when you hear that there is a TV special on the wonders of the United States which will include a visual tour of the Grand Canyon, you take time to see it for yourself. This experience heightens your realization of what it is like to see and feel the effects of the Canyon in comparison with the rest of the landscape of Arizona. You know that it is a breathtaking experience to walk up to it, look down into its depths, scan the miles of its formations, and realize that God made it all. You know that people have gotten lost in it, they have explored it for decades, and still they are learning its secrets and treasures.

This process can help us understand part of why we struggle with a proper view of God. Even if we believe the Bible, we often do so with mental assent and not with a heart-felt realization of what the truths about God mean to us. We know he is omnipresent, omniscient, and all-powerful. But is that *real* to us? We must experience this reality in our lives. This, however, is a *faith experience*. We learn these things to be true by faith. Nonetheless, such an experience can be just as powerful as seeing something like the Grand Canyon. Yet too

---

What is it in our culture that so demeans God and affects us so that we are not in personal worship of Him?

_____

_____

_____

_____

_____

_____

_____

_____

What kind of commitment do you think you need to make in order to have personal, private, and glorious worship of your God?

_____

_____

_____

_____

_____

_____

_____

What would you say hinders you, schedule-wise, the most?

_____

_____

_____

_____

_____

_____

What are your thoughts as you meditate on God's greatness?

_____
_____
_____
_____
_____
_____
_____
_____
_____
_____
_____
_____
_____
_____

Which is your favorite Scripture passage that describes that greatness of God? Write a paragraph based on this passage about His glory.

_____
_____
_____
_____
_____
_____
_____
_____
_____
_____
_____
_____
_____

often, what we know of God has little impact on our inner being, our hearts. Thus, when the world offers us thrills that touch us deeply, we sense those events and savor their influence on our souls much more profoundly than we do God and truth about Him, which seem to affect us minimally or superficially. *So the world's substitutes for God begin to have a greater hold on us, and God's presence and attributes, His offer of peace, safety, glory, and satisfaction, make little impression on us.*

Therefore, we need to learn to meditate on the nature and attributes of our God. We must practice the reality of the Holy Spirit's presence and power in our lives in some way so that we cannot get away from His daily touch. We need to consider the glory, beauty, worthiness, and virtues of our God so that, as Jonathan Edwards once said, they move "our affections most sensibly and strongly. How great cause have we therefore to be humbled to the dust, that we are no more affected!"[2] He was right!

We are not affected, touched, moved, or impressed inwardly as we should be in the realms of our desires, ambitions, appetites, ardor, aspirations, and cravings. How can we change this? Just as we need the direct impact of the Grand Canyon's wonder to touch our senses, so we need the direct touch of God's glory on our hearts. *This can only come as we spend time daily, weekly, and regularly thinking on what the Word says about Him.*

PSALM 29: A CALL TO ADORE GOD
Most of this psalm is a picture of God's glory and power. Read it and use it as a template for expressing your adoration of God, following it with the exercise below in meditating on God. You will then be on your way to developing or cultivating a heart that enjoys thoughts of God.

EXERCISE IN MEDITATION ON GOD

We need big thoughts and big words to describe a great God. Below is a list of adjectives and nouns that extend our feeble, normal language in expressing thoughts about God. Use them to help you meditate on God.

- *awesome:* astonishing, awe-inspiring, beautiful, breathtaking, daunting, dreadful, exalted, formidable, grand, imposing, impressive, intimidating, magnificent, majestic, mind-blowing, moving, overwhelming, shocking, striking, stunning, stupefying, wonderful, wondrous
- *splendor:* brightness, brilliance, ceremony, dazzle, display, effulgence, gorgeousness, grandeur, luster, magnificence
- *elegance:* majesty, pageantry, pomp, radiance, refulgence, renown, resplendence, reverence, richness, solemnity, spectacle, stateliness
- *magnificence:* class, dignity, distinction, exquisiteness, grandeur, hauteur, nobility, splendor
- *glory:* dignity, distinction, eminence, exaltation, fame, grandeur, greatness, honor, illustriousness, magnificence, majesty, nobility, praise, prestige, renown, reputation, splendor, sublimity
- *exquisite:* admirable, attractive, beautiful, charming, choice, comely, consummate, elegant, ethereal, fastidious, fine, flawless, impeccable, incomparable, irreproachable, lovely, matchless, meticulous, outstanding, peerless, perfect, pleasing, polished, precious, precise, rare, splendid, striking, superb, superior, superlative
- *incomparable:* excellent, exceptional, inimitable, matchless, paramount, peerless, perfect, preeminent, sovereign, superior, supreme, surpassing,

Small groups: What are your ideas about the worship of God? Is this hard for you? Does the world around you make it hard for you to focus on God's majesty?

_____

_____

_____

_____

_____

_____

_____

_____

_____

_____

_____

_____

_____

Transcendence. Write down what you think it means that God is "high and lifted up."

_____

_____

_____

_____

_____

_____

_____

_____

_____

_____

_____

Your thoughts on Isaiah 57:15:

Focus on the cross:

towering, transcendent, ultimate, unequalled, unmatchable, unmatched, unparalleled, unrivalled, unsurpassable

God is incomparable. To what can we liken Him? He is incomparable in His greatness. He is incomparable in His might and power. He is incomparable in His importance; everything exists solely because of Him. He is also beyond comparison in His love and pity, and He is unequalled in His grace, surpassing all in His kindness toward those whom He must condescend even to look upon.

God is all-powerful. He is powerful in His creation of the world and in His power over nature. He displayed His power when Christ conquered the grave through His resurrection; He promises that same resurrection power to His children. He illustrated His power when he created the world in six days, when He divided the Red Sea, and when He brought the plagues upon Egypt.

God is awesome. He is awesome in His grace. His glory is awesome. He is awesome in His might and power. The awesome reality of God's presence is overwhelming to the soul. Consider the astonishing might of God. He is mighty, incredibly and breathtakingly awesome in the power of His Word. All creation responds to His Word toward the end God desires. This might and strength of our God is unmatched and intimidating. We stand in wonder at the restraint God shows toward puny, wicked, and rebellious sinners who can be wiped out by His mind-blowing power. The display of His power is seen in a storm, with the wind and the waves, or through the moving of huge, man-made structures that are like matchsticks in the hands of God.

Why is it so hard for us to worship God? Why does it take such work to give God the glory He so richly deserves? We must bow before Him in awe and wonder. We cannot give more to God than He already has, but we can recognize His power and majesty, and lift up His incomparable glory and marvelous splendor to the world around us. But how can we do this? Only after we have been moved in our hearts by the imposing radiance of His person. And when will we do this? We are so busy in our service and ministry. Our schedule of duties and works is overcrowded. We tend to be full of our sense of our greatness and gifts, and moved by our own abilities and personal traits—so much so that we cannot begin to appreciate how much higher and more noble is our God. The sacred awe due to our God is lost in the homage we give to man.

- The infinite excellence and glorious transcendence of our God is lost on us; we miss their effect on our lives.
- We are too busy doing spiritual work for God to allow His supremacy to move us. We are serving God, but we don't have time to think about Him.
- We can even preach about Him, but we do not really know the consummate resplendence of His person.
- We must stop and be still. We must get alone and stop the ministry merry-go-round long enough to be affected by the dazzling display of His immanent holiness.
- We must know God! He "inhabits eternity" (Isa. 57:15), and yet He will come and dwell with those who will take the time to come to Him with a meek and contrite spirit.
- What would you have to cut out if you desired to spend real time alone with God? How much time would you have to reserve?

Notes

1 Music and words by **Bob Kauflin** © 2006 Sovereign Grace Praise (BMI). www.SovereignGraceMusic.org. Used with permission.

2 "Is there anything which Christians can find in heaven or earth, so worthy to be the objects of their admiration and love, their earnest and longing desires, their hope, and their rejoicing, and their fervent zeal, as those things that are held forth to us in the gospel of Jesus Christ? In which not only are things declared most worthy to affect us, but they are exhibited in the most affecting manner. The glory and beauty of the blessed Jehovah, which is most worthy in itself, to be the object of our admiration and love, is there exhibited in the most affecting manner that can be conceived of, as it appears, shining in all its luster, in the face of an incarnate, infinitely loving, meek, compassionate, dying Redeemer ... So has God disposed things, in the affair of our redemption, and in his glorious dispensations, revealed to us in the gospel, as though everything were purposely contrived in such a manner, as to have the greatest possible tendency to reach our hearts in the most tender part, and move our affections most sensibly and strongly," **Jonathan Edwards**, *Religious Affections*, Part 1.III.3; quoted at www.leaderu.com/cyber/books/religaffect/rapt1sec3.html; accessed June 2012.

Day 7. Focus on the Cross

God thoughts:

Focus on the cross:

Our focus today is the Via Delorosa, the path Christ followed as He went to the cross. We may not often meditate on this part of the Passion of Christ, but we should consider what it was like for Him to have gone through all the previous physical and emotional stress, along with the shame, and now to move from that trauma into the streets of Jerusalem.

Up to this point He has been handled by the priests and the Roman soldiers. Now he will be exposed to the anger and filth of the Jewish crowds gathered for the event. The Jewish leaders have made sure that the crowd is sufficiently stirred up and supportive of their intent to crucify Christ. Now He will travel up the road to Golgotha. His back is ripped to repulsive shreds. His body is beaten and bruised. Yet He is compelled to carry His cross (John 19:17). How far He gets before Simon takes over this task we are not sure. The text does not tell us. But Jesus's body is being pushed to the limits of human pain and shame.

It is not hard to imagine the faces of the Roman soldiers as they sneer at this prisoner, supposedly a guilty man who has been rejected by His own people. The Romans care little for such men. The Jews themselves have been whipped into a frenzy that is about to culminate in a crucifixion that is without doubt their desired end for this man who has so plagued their country. Do some spit on Him as he passes? Do others call out and add to His pain and shame by calling for Him to defend Himself? The path is hard. The walk is long. Jesus has been up all night, being attacked verbally, physically, and spiritually. He is now approaching the moment He could see coming when He bowed in prayer to His Father in Gethsemane. Christ knows He must endure

130

more than just the crowd and the pain. He is not yet done. He knows that His death will not come quickly with a sword or a spear, but that He is about to endure the most agonizing form of death known to that world. And most of all, He knows that the sin and guilt of all His people is about to be placed on Him. As the God-Man, He will experience something that is impossible to explain. This is what is going through His mind as He approaches Calvary.

Daily Meditation Theme

- *Greatness of God:* "In my distress I called upon the LORD; to my God I cried for help. From his temple he heard my voice, and my cry to him reached his ears. Then the earth reeled and rocked; the foundations also of the mountains trembled and quaked, because he was angry. Smoke went up from his nostrils, and devouring fire from his mouth; glowing coals flamed forth from him. He bowed the heavens and came down; thick darkness was under his feet. He rode on a cherub and flew; he came swiftly on the wings of the wind. He made darkness his covering, his canopy around him, thick clouds dark with water. Out of the brightness before him hailstones and coals of fire broke through his clouds. The LORD also thundered in the heavens, and the Most High uttered his voice, hailstones and coals of fire. And he sent out his arrows and scattered them; he flashed forth lightnings and routed them. Then the channels of the sea were seen, and the foundations of the world were laid bare at your rebuke, O LORD, at the blast of the breath of your nostrils" (Ps. 18:6–15).

Song: "O To See the Dawn"

Oh to see the dawn of the darkest day;
Christ on the road to Calvary:
Tried by sinful men, torn and beaten then,
Nailed to a cross of wood.

Oh to see the pain written on your face,
Bearing the awesome weight of sin.
Every bitter thought, every evil deed ,
Crowning Your blood-stained brow.

This the power of the cross, Christ became sin for us;
Took the blame bore the wrath; we stand forgiven at the cross

Now the daylight flees, now the ground beneath,
Quakes as its Maker bows his head,
Curtain torn in two, dead are raised to life,
'Finished' the victory cry.

How does this song help you meditate on God's goodness?

_____
_____
_____
_____
_____
_____
_____
_____
_____
_____
_____
_____
_____
_____

What do you see in Psalm 18?

_____
_____
_____
_____
_____
_____
_____
_____
_____
_____
_____
_____
_____
_____
_____
_____
_____
_____
_____

Oh, to see my name written in the wounds,
For through Your suffering I am free.
Death is crushed to death, life is mine to live,
Won through Your selfless love.

Final Chorus:

*This the power of the cross, Son of God, slain for us.
What a love, what a cost; we stand forgiven at the cross.* [1]

Note

1 Keith Getty and Stuart Townend, 2005. Thankyou Music. EMI Christian Music Publishing.

Week 5.
Walk with Your God

Replacing the *cheap pleasure* of this world with the *deep treasure* of God's glory.

What are we satisfied with in our culture? What are we seeking in our churches? What is it that our families are living for? One of the main reasons that we go to the "slop trough" of this world for a little sensual pleasure is that we have never really come to enjoy the pleasure of a close walk with God. In fact, we are not even sure what a deep, intimate relationship with Him would be like. We are satisfied with a social event called "church" rather than a relationship with people who *are* the church. We are satisfied with a spiritual activity called "religion" rather than a real, vibrant relationship with an all-powerful God. But God made us for so much more. We need to get a glimpse of what it is like to enjoy the glory of God up close and personal on a daily basis. This deep treasure offered to us will then replace the cheap pleasure the world offers.

Day 1. Intimacy with God: Introduction

God thoughts:

_____
_____
_____
_____
_____
_____
_____
_____
_____
_____
_____
_____
_____
_____
_____
_____
_____
_____
_____
_____
_____
_____
_____
_____
_____
_____
_____
_____
_____
_____
_____
_____
_____
_____
_____

Daily Meditation Themes

- *Goodness of God:* "For I am sure that neither death nor life, nor angels nor rulers, nor things present nor things to come, nor powers, nor height nor depth, nor anything else in all creation, will be able to separate us from the love of God in Christ Jesus our Lord" (Rom. 8:38–39).
- *Greatness of God:* "Ascribe to the LORD, O heavenly beings, ascribe to the LORD glory and strength. Ascribe to the LORD the glory due his name; worship the LORD in the splendor of holiness. The voice of the LORD is over the waters; the God of glory thunders … The voice of the LORD is powerful; the voice of the LORD is full of majesty. The voice of the LORD breaks the cedars … The voice of the LORD flashes forth flames of fire. The voice of the LORD shakes the wilderness … The voice of the LORD makes the deer give birth and strips the forests bare, and in his temple all cry, 'Glory!' The LORD sits enthroned over the flood; the LORD sits enthroned as king forever. May the LORD give strength to his people! May the LORD bless his people with peace!" (Ps. 29).

Song: "Above All Powers"

Above all powers, above all kings
Above all nature and all created things
Above all wisdom and all the ways of man
You were here, before the world began
Above all kingdoms, above all thrones
Above all wonders the world has ever known
Above all wealth and treasures of the earth
There's no way to measure what You're worth

Crucified, laid behind a stone
You lived to die, rejected and alone

Like a rose, trampled on the ground
You took the fall and thought of me
Above all[1]

Meditation

This week we will look at our need for a deep walk with God. Although earlier I alluded to this in general terms, we will now look specifically at what this kind of relationship looks like. In America and all the countries where technology is readily available, I think that this is probably one of the most needed concepts in twenty-first-century Christianity. This generation—and perhaps part of the previous one—has had numerous Christian benefits poured upon on it. Many teens, college students, and young adults have known the blessing of Christian schools, families, and home schooling. They have known their parents' provision for their daily lives. They have had plenty of teaching and preaching about what is right and wrong. Few have had to stand up for their beliefs or convictions.

Yet little has been done to direct such young people to a full experience of walking with God. They know that in order to be a Bible kind of Christian you must have a relationship with God before you have a relationship with church people. They have a concept of a relationship with a Savior and Master, but they have heard or learned little about having a relationship with God that is deep and intimate, as with a friend. If they have heard of God spoken of as a friend, it has been too much in the sense of a common or popular "buddy"; it is not a relationship with the God and King who can be my closest friend. To have a casual relationship with God is like taking a $10 bill when you are offered a lifetime supply of $1,000 bills.

So how can we develop that kind of intimacy with God? Does the Bible suggest that this is possible or necessary? There are two biblical

Women: describe any struggles you face in forming lasting, deep relationships.

Small groups: Have you been hurt in a relationship or friendship? If so, discuss how that has affected your desire to look for further deep relationships.

What is it about God that motivates you to develop a deeper relationship with Him?

Did you find hindrances in your home to your having deep relationships as you grew up?

_____

_____

_____

_____

_____

_____

Who has best demonstrated to you how to have a more intimate relationship on the human level?

_____

_____

_____

_____

Small groups: How would you describe your relationship with God? Make a list of adjectives.

_____

_____

_____

_____

What is the closest you have come to having a deep friendship or relationship? Describe it.

_____

_____

_____

_____

concepts that convey to us that God wants an intimate, deep relationship or friendship with us, rather than a casual, courteous one.

The first is that God made us in His image. We considered this truth last week. This act set us apart from the rest of His creation. He does not have a personal relationship with the animals; He is the Creator and they are His creation. They do not worship Him; man does. God made us like Himself so that we could know Him on a personal level. We are to be like Him.

Paul presents us with the second truth in Ephesians 5:22–35. He parallels two relationships in order to help us understand the commitment made and needed in them both. He says that Christ gave Himself for the church (v. 25). He is the Head of the church. In a similar way, the husband is the head of the wife and should give himself for her. Every wife wants her husband to love her and know her. She hopes that he will be a man who will share his life with her. In fact, "sharing" is the key verb that describes an intimate relationship with someone. These two relationships, then—that between Christ and the church and a husband and his wife—are similar and comparable.

Genesis 1–3 glues these two concepts together. Here we see God communing with the man He has created. God's people were made naked and open to Him, and they were not only unashamed, but they also enjoyed this intimacy of knowledge and experience with God. He knew them and they knew each other. There were no hidden agendas, no areas of the heart that were withheld from one another. This is the kind of relationship God made us for.

A husband and wife *share four beautiful aspects of life*: their *time*, their *themes* (desires, goals, dreams), their *treasures*, and their *thrills* (life experiences). The more they share in these areas, the deeper their commitment, trust, care and love will grow. They will feel increasingly that they know each other down to the smallest details of their thoughts and hopes, likes and dislikes. However, there are people who have lived together for years and share very little. They have their own bank accounts, personal cars, separate work and careers; they go to different events, they only occasionally have a nice meal together, they may have kids (which become "his/hers" when they are bad and "mine" when they excel), and while they go on vacation together, they like to do separate activities there. They have the same house for the sake of tax purposes and for appearances (perhaps to their church), but they do not share much else. It is much easier for them to go through life enduring the family structure while enjoying their personal lives apart from the family. In fact, they find as much time as possible to get away from home in order to enjoy what they like, and only occasionally spend time as needed with their spouse and the family. This picture describes far too many households in the twenty-first-century church.

What does this kind of couple know about a deep and personal relationship with God? How would men and women living like this go about developing or sharing their lives with God? If we were to describe their relationship with God, we might use terms such as "convenient" (He is there when they need Him), "casual" (they talk to Him when it is socially acceptable and spiritually necessary), "ornamental" (they like to know that God does meet with them in church), "mechanical" (they go through the motions of prayer and spiritual activities because it is expected of them), and "miserable" (some endure it just long enough to get something more interesting than what the world has to offer—in other words, they do not even know Christ as Savior). The adjectives

Can you be together with others in a group setting without checking your cell phone for text messages? Can you actually switch it off, or do you feel the "need" to know if someone wants you? Does this make you feel powerful or needed? Do you find your focus in social media rather than in the person sitting next to you?

Small groups: Discuss how technology has connected us but also contributed to shallowness in our relationships.

Final observations:
_____
_____
_____
_____
_____
_____
_____
_____
_____
_____
_____
_____
_____
_____
_____
_____
_____
_____
_____
_____
_____
_____
_____
_____
_____
_____
_____
_____
_____
_____
_____
_____
_____
_____
_____
_____

"deep," "intimate," "fervent," "meaningful," and "profound" would not describe their relationship with God or perhaps anyone in their vicinity. They are too busy talking on their cell phones to people in business 2,000 miles away, listening to a podcast, or checking the last twenty-five emails from their broker or friends in school, to talk to the person sitting across the table and get to know what he or she is like.

It may be time for us to "disconnect" from our electronic means of communication so that we can "connect" with those closest to us and find out what is going on with them. But most importantly, we need to find out what a direct, personal, and intimate (knowing me completely) relationship is like. I used to "do" Christianity until I finally started focusing on "being" and knowing God directly, and I would never go back to the plastic form of Christianity. It stinks. It is like Charlie Brown's teacher—you never know what she is saying but she serves a purpose in the cartoon. That is what God and our Christianity is like all too often. It serves a purpose, but we don't get too involved.

Before we end, let me address men. For the most part, we seem to be more driven to "do" things in life, in order to produce, to perform, and to achieve. Work is our main focus. Guys go through high school and enter college with limited depth in relationships. Many men have not been encouraged to get into conversations beyond intellectual talk about science and nature, sports, music performance, and so on. We celebrate the achievements of others—what they have "done."

During college years we rarely spend time sitting and talking about what we *are* inside. If your parents say that your friend is struggling and having troubles in life, you might reply that they are wrong, because you talked to him earlier today and he is fine, things are fine, and his life is OK. The only thing troubling him is that his favorite sports team lost to a real "loser" of a team that is at the bottom of the division. That was bad.

To suggest that something is going on inside your friend's heart seems weird to you. He's OK, as far as you know. Men don't talk about their fears and struggles. We rarely find out what others are thinking or observing. This must change. How will we develop an intimate relationship with God, the invisible and glorious King, when we do little to develop a depth in our daily relationships?

Women are way ahead of us in this department. Their struggle is different. They tend to develop relationships quickly, based on feelings and likes. Then, if they have an argument, they tend to move on to another relationship with someone else. Girls tend to be up and down, and they struggle to leave their feelings aside in order to know someone and help him or her become a better person. The depth of their relationships is therefore questionable as well.

Women talk more together and so they know more about one another. However, what they do with that knowledge and relationship is often not helpful to their walk with God. They treat God the same way. When He does not fit their plan or agree with their ways, they move on to a human relationship, instead of adjusting themselves to God. They look for support and encouragement from others to stroke their egos and feelings.

Note

1 **Lenny LaBlanc and Paul Baloche,** 1999. Integrity's Hosanna! Music. EMI Christian Music Publishing (IMI) LenSongs Publishing, Inc.

Day 2. Intimacy with God (1)

God thoughts:
_____
_____
_____
_____
_____
_____
_____
_____
_____
_____
_____
_____
_____
_____
_____
_____
_____
_____
_____
_____
_____
_____
_____
_____
_____
_____
_____
_____
_____
_____
_____
_____
_____

Daily Meditation Themes

- *Goodness of God:* "Now may our Lord Jesus Christ himself, and God our Father, who loved us and gave us eternal comfort and good hope through grace, comfort yourhearts and establish them in every good work and word" (2 Thes. 2:16–17).
- *Greatness of God:* "By the word of the LORD the heavens were made, and by the breath of his mouth all their host. He gathers the waters of the sea as a heap; he puts the deeps in storehouses. Let all the earth fear the LORD; let all the inhabitants of the world stand in awe of him!" (Ps. 33:6–8).

Song: "Am I A Soldier of the Cross?"

Am I a soldier of the cross—
A follower of the Lamb?
And shall I fear to own His cause,
Or blush to speak His name?

Must I be carried to the skies
On flowery beds of ease,
While others fought to win the prize
And sailed through bloody seas?

Are there no foes for me to face?
Must I not stem the flood?
Is this vile world a friend to grace,
To help me on to God?

Sure I must fight if I would reign,
Increase my courage, Lord!
I'll bear the toil, endure the pain,
Supported by Thy Word.[1]

Meditation

Yesterday we saw that a husband and wife share four beautiful aspects of life. Today and for the next three days we will consider each of these in turn and apply them to an intimate relationship with God. The first aspect is:

WE SHARE TIME

When a man and a woman commit themselves to the deeper relationship of marriage, they will spend time together. Without this, it is not possible for them to have more than a surface relationship. But what do they do with this time? Is it spent *doing things*? Perhaps. However, the most powerful way of spending time together is in communication, so that we not only share time in the same place and doing the same things, but more importantly we share ourselves. We listen and we speak so that we can understand and care.

With God, this kind of sharing happens in private, in quiet meetings alone with Him. That can be hard. We don't know what to do with God alone. We lack the desire to read His Word and listen to what He says. We can get into the study-and-achieve mode when it comes to God's Word. We want to get an A or a ribbon because we can recite large portions of it or regurgitate the right answers about it. But we don't grasp that this Word is what God has *said*. He spoke. We must listen. We are to be listeners and learners so that we can enjoy our relationship with Him. Parents, pastors, and educators, please find a way to change your focus and use of the Bible so that it is less a book to be tested about and mainly a book to be loved and read through for its ability to help us all know God more intimately.

Then we should follow this time with talking to God about what He has said about Himself, His will, His plan, and His people. Talk to God. Do you have anything worthwhile to say to Him? At the very least, you can talk to God about Himself. For those who have grown up in Christianity there is a special need to

Small groups: Discuss how difficult it is to spend time alone with someone you care about. Now apply this to spending time with God.

Write down your desire to know God through prayer.

How does faith need to grow with the time you spend in prayer?

Small groups: What do you think will help you become more real as you talk to God in prayer?

appreciate God for who He is and what He has done. Apathy is our curse. We have grown accustomed to what we know about God. It does not move us deeply. We must spend time daily in prayer or song *with our hearts engaged* in deep gratitude for, and worship of, God's greatness and work on our behalf. This helps deepen our relationship with Him. As often as possible, we must review what Christ did on the cross, and do this in such a way that it moves our affections in gratefulness for His sacrifice and suffering. Preach the gospel to yourself regularly.

But wait. I said that this first aspect of sharing involves time. There is the problem. We spend five minutes in prayer and feel that we have prayed a lot. We spend five or ten minutes in the Bible and we find that we cannot concentrate on the truth for any more time. Our interest and thoughts wander away from this meeting with God.

Men, imagine being with your wife or girlfriend. You are sitting at a table with her and she is talking, but your eyes wander to other things around you. Your attention is drawn to the other things you can see and hear. Your mind is not engaged in knowing her and your emotions and affections are not engaged in enjoying her presence. She notices and asks you a question to get you to focus back on her. Perhaps she asks you about something she just said, and this embarrasses you because you don't have any idea what she has been talking about. But if you *really care* about what she is saying and you *really want to know her thoughts and heart desires*, you will stay focused on her. You will passionately and intensely focus on her words and will be motivated to get their meaning.

I think the same is true about God. When you have the opportunity to sit down and take in what He has said and you really care about it, you will stay focused. You will desire to understand and you will be motivated to get His meaning. The time will go by quickly while you are absorbed in meeting with and seeking to know God. Hours can fly by when spent in the presence of one we love and care deeply about. Should we be regimented or mechanical about the amount of time we spend with God and say that a "spiritual" person will spend an hour with God while a carnal one will spend no more time than just a few minutes? No. But the reverse is certainly true. You cannot spend five minutes with God daily and know Him personally and intimately. When Christians *want* to spend time in God's presence, they don't pay attention to the time. (I once heard a speaker say that it is amazing how people get uptight about expecting believers to set apart time in God's His Word. If they spend thirty minutes out of the 1,440 they live per day; this isn't even 5 percent of their day.)

The average twenty-first-century prayer life consists of a series of brief "Hi, God" type prayers: thanks for the food; help me with my exam; please help my mom's sister, who is in trouble; take care of the missionaries and bless them; be with somebody somewhere today who needs something. We talk to God in the same way we talk to folk about the weather. Our communication is necessary but not deep; only as it concerns or changes our plans does it become important to us.

There is one more problem with this whole concept of developing intimacy with God. We do not *see* Him. This is a faith relationship. You may ask, How can I delight in and enjoy a relationship with someone I have never seen? You only feel that you are talking to someone when you can see him or her. But what is it about not seeing Him that you struggle with? Do you want to know the color of His eyes? Do you want to know the shape of His face?

What is your relationship with God like? Describe it.

_____
_____
_____
_____
_____
_____
_____
_____
_____
_____
_____

Small groups: Share with one another the hindrances you find in journaling about God and His Word.

_____
_____
_____
_____
_____
_____
_____
_____
_____
_____
_____
_____
_____
_____

But with God, you get to know His shape and size through the pages of His Word. Your eyes of faith must be overwhelmed by His majesty and glory in every way. I can delight in this God. I begin to see Him clearly and gloriously through the pages of Scripture.

Prayer is faith's twin brother. Faith moves me to talk to the One I have begun to know through the Bible. I enjoy this time in prayer because we have so much to talk about. I get away from the distractions of life so that I can focus on God and my relationship with Him.

In 2 Corinthians 3:18 Paul suggests to us that the more time we spend exposed to the glory of God, the more we will reflect this glory and the character of God. Spend time with God. Enjoy Him. He will change you forever.

And, finally, make the time you spend in God's Word time spent with Him. Journal your thoughts about God. Make Him the center of your reading and meditation. The CCPP pattern can help you: look in Scripture for God's *Commands*, God's *Character*, God's *Promises*, and God's *People* (see Appendix 2 for an example of this). Whatever you are learning as you read will always give you a connection point to God, not just information about history.

Note

1 **Isaac Watts,** 1721–1724.

Day 3. Intimacy with God (2)

Daily Meditation Themes

- *Goodness of God:* "And God is able to make all grace abound to you, so that, having all sufficiency in all things at all times, you may abound in every good work" (2 Cor. 9:8).
- *Greatness of God:* "You have multiplied, O LORD my God, your wondrous deeds and your thoughts toward us; none can compare with you! I will proclaim and tell of them, yet they are more than can be told" (Ps 40:5).

Song: "Lord, You're All I Need"

Oft times I've tried to live my life
According to my will;
When darkness comes it's difficult
To rest and just be still.
But Lord, You are my Shepherd
That guides me in the way,
And I will learn this glorious truth
If I Your Word obey.

You're all I need.
You're the Lord of everything.
All I need.
This is why I humbly sing.
Your strength is sustaining
And Your grace has made me free.
You're my heart's lone desire,
You're all I need.

By wanting more I've wanted less
Than all You've given me.
You gave Your all by laying down
Your life at Calvary.
So I surrender all, Lord,
My best to you I give,

How is God portrayed in these passages?

_____
_____
_____
_____
_____
_____
_____
_____
_____
_____
_____
_____
_____
_____
_____
_____
_____
_____
_____
_____
_____
_____
_____
_____
_____
_____
_____
_____
_____
_____
_____
_____
_____
_____

What have you experienced with God by faith thus far? Can you testify to the wonder and glory of knowing that God has definitely taken you through life situations that brought you closer to Him?

Small groups: What personal desires, goals, and dreams do you think you need to change to allow for God's priorities to find place in your heart?

And thank You now for giving me
A reason to live.[1]

Meditation

Today we come to the second beautiful aspect of an intimate relationship with God:

WE SHARE THE SAME THEMES (DESIRES, GOALS, DREAMS)

The more time a couple spends together, the more they begin to think alike. Each adjusts his or her plans and hopes to complement those of the other person. They find common pursuits that allow them to accomplish their goals. They sacrifice personal time and energy in order to see these common dreams become a reality. The time they spend together helps them understand each other's perspective and thinking. They find that they are headed in the same direction: what drives them is similar and they have a common purpose.

On our twenty-fifth anniversary my wife and I took a trip to Canada. We had been talking about this for about two or three years and had discussed different options for making great memories together. We wanted it to be a special event in our journey of marriage and life. For many months before our trip, we both cut back on our expenses in order to finance it. We planned, talked, and laid down what we would like to do together. To achieve this goal we set aside plans to visit other places, such as Europe and different parts of America. We planned to visit Calgary, Alberta, and Vancouver. We were agreed on and excited about the plans. As different parts of the trip came together, we were both motivated to keep on target, financially and logistically. Even the fact that our two daughters were headed for Africa on a short-term missions trip during the same period did not detract us from our plans.

How about our relationship with God? Do

we share His plans, dreams, goals, and purposes for this world? Are we interested in hearing about and understanding what God wants to do in His church? Do we adjust our thinking and priorities to reflect God's priorities? Have we spent time meditating on what God has said to His church and how it should change our lives? Is His holy character reflected in ours? We are back to the concept of time with God that has meaning and depth. Are we surrendered to His will?

In Galatians 2:20–21 Paul said, "I have been crucified with Christ. It is no longer I who live, but Christ who lives in me. And the life I now live in the flesh I live by faith in the Son of God, who loved me and gave himself for me. I do not nullify the grace of God, for if righteousness were through the law, then Christ died for no purpose." Think about these verses. Paul had one focus, and that was Christ. Whatever Christ wanted, Paul wanted. He was willing to put all other things aside for what Christ needed from his life. We need this kind of relationship with Christ. We need Paul's intense focus of Philippians 3:10–14, where he says, "one thing I do …" We need to catch the drift of God's direction.

What are God's main goals?

HIS GLORY

If we share this goal with God, life becomes a one-track system, headed for whatever brings the most glory to God (1 Cor. 10:31). Do I share this concern for God's glory? Do I care about whether the glory goes to God or not? When I live a good or righteous life, am I wondering whether people pay attention, or do I just hope that it has brought fame to His name? When I am investing in the lives of a lost world, am I wondering who is watching, or am I wondering whether people will understand that God has done the miraculous?

Small groups: Make a list of eternal values. Discuss them with one another.

_____

_____

_____

_____

_____

_____

_____

What drives your life? What do you give the most time to? What matters the most to you?

_____

_____

_____

_____

_____

How would people around you answer those questions? What evidence do you find for this?

_____

_____

_____

_____

_____

_____

_____

_____

_____

_____

_____

Why has the 21st-century believer strayed so far from these themes so dear and important to God?

_____

_____

_____

_____

_____

_____

_____

_____

_____

_____

_____

_____

_____

Small groups: Who is on your list of lost people you are praying for? What have you done sacrificially to bring them to Christ?

_____

_____

_____

_____

_____

_____

_____

_____

_____

_____

_____

_____

_____

_____

ETERNAL VALUES

This is the big picture for God. Do I have eternal values in my mind? As I live and go through troubles and problems, do I wonder why they happen to me, or do I wonder how God will work them out in eternity? If I don't understand all that happens to me, do I rest in God's big plan? Am I pouring myself into things that will matter for eternity, or do I pour my time, energies, and money into things that will burn? People, both unsaved and in the body of Christ, will last for eternity.

The Word of God and His promises will never fail. They are eternal. Do I demonstrate this in my life? Are the most important plans in my life eternal ones? Our greatest priority is to become like Christ (Rom. 8:28–29). This is God's purpose for every believer. If I run my plans and activities, my friends, family, fun, and finances through the grid of God's purpose to make me like Christ, my honest and humble response may be that I need to change some things. Matthew 6:20 says that we are to "lay up for [ourselves] treasures in heaven." Do it. Don't accumulate things and build empires here that will burn and be useless in eternity.

HIS BRIDE, THE CHURCH

Christ began to build His church while here on this earth. He prepared the foundation, the apostles, so that they could launch a worldwide work of reaching the lost and establishing local bodies of believers. Do I care about the church? Do I give myself to help my local church grow and flourish? Do I care about what goes on there? Do I want to encourage the body of believers and love them unconditionally, as does Christ? Do I attempt to keep focused on what God will do for the good of His body? Do my plans and dreams for life revolve around the body of Christ and my local church, or do I allow the world system to attract my heart's loves and affections?

God loves the church and sacrificed Himself for it. What is my attitude toward the body of believers God has brought together in my church? If I spend time getting to know God's plan for showing the world His love and holy character, I will realize that it flows through His church.

THE LOST

How can we come to know the purpose and plan of God without seeing His heart for the ungodly world of people headed for eternity in hell?

His eternal purpose has been to redeem to Himself a people from all tribes and tongues. He wants His glory to be spread throughout the world as we know it. His power to change lives must invade the darkness across the world and explode in the light of His glory.

I hope you want to be a part of that plan. Spend time with God. Read His Word. Catch His heart for eternal life, for saving men and women, and for His majesty, power, and glory spread through all the nations, tribes, and peoples. Sharing these drives will be evidence of a new depth of intimacy in your relationship with God. People will see something different in you. Your life will look different because your heart passion will be for God's work, not your fame.

Note

1 **James Tilson.** Copied by permission of The WILDS. All rights reserved.

Day 4. Intimacy with God (3)

God thoughts:

_____
_____
_____
_____
_____
_____
_____
_____
_____
_____
_____
_____
_____
_____
_____
_____
_____
_____
_____
_____
_____
_____
_____
_____
_____
_____
_____
_____
_____
_____
_____
_____
_____
_____
_____
_____
_____

Daily Meditation Themes

- *Goodness of God:* "Rejoice in the Lord, O you righteous, and give thanks to his holy name!" (Ps. 97:12). "Thanks be to God for his inexpressible gift!" (2 Cor. 9:15).
- *Greatness of God:* "In God we have boasted continually, and we will give thanks to your name forever" (Ps. 44:8).

Song: "Lord of My Heart"

Jesus, eternal Jehovah,
King of the heavens you are.
Loving and caring, forgiving,
You are the Lord of my heart.

Lord of my heart, Savior divine,
You shed your blood, suffered, and died,
Giving me life, You gave your all,
Lord of my heart.

Jesus, my wonderful Savior,
King of all Kings, Ruler on high.
Lord of all glory forever,
You are the Lord of my life.

Jesus, my Rock of salvation,
my Refuge, my Fortress, my God,
Hope of the Lord for all nations,
You are the Lord of my life.

Jesus, bright Son of the Father,
You came to die in my place;
I see you hanging on Calv'ry,
You are the Lord of my heart.

Jesus, alone on Golgotha,
Bearing my grief and my shame,
Smitten by God and afflicted,
You bore the sins of my heart.[1]

Meditation

Today we come to the third beautiful aspect of an intimate relationship:

WE SHARE OUR TREASURES

Consider the following: gifts, abilities, houses, family, kids, life, money. The key concept here is trust. The more we deepen our relationship with someone, the more we trust them with what we have and what we are.

Before their marriage, a man and woman will spend time together sharing their thoughts, beliefs, and goals. When these things seem to line up and when they find each other to be trustworthy, they begin to share their inner feelings, fears, and cares. They have found someone who will not laugh at them. They care about the same things. Then they share themselves totally. Their marriage is a commitment to sharing everything they have with each other. They can trust each other with their house, their car, and their money. They will be willing to share in the raising of children that are their joint heritage. They do not wonder whether they *should* share these things.

What do we trust God with? Do we know that God will use our gifts for His eternal purposes? Are we happy to give all that we have to Him? This trust can only come out of our relationship with Him.

I don't question what my wife will do with our finances. Should I question what God will do with them through the local church? I should be willing to give everything to Him. His will is "good and acceptable and perfect" (Rom. 12:2).

Think about this: even if I don't understand what God is doing with one of my children or with some portion of my life, it is still OK. I

What treasure does this world offer that is hard for you to entrust to God?

_____

_____

_____

_____

_____

_____

_____

_____

_____

_____

Small groups: Has God taken away from you something or someone you valued? Does the loss of that treasure matter more to you than God does?

_____

_____

_____

_____

_____

_____

_____

_____

_____

_____

_____

_____

_____

trust Him. That kind of faith in God will be made a reality through the events God brings into our lives.

Do I think I can work out my life better? Do I believe I deserve a trouble-free life in which all my "stuff" is never destroyed and all my family is never in trouble or harmed? The problem with that kind of "ideal" life is that it lacks one key component. The American Dream lacks the Kingdom of God. I can lose everything for His sake, as long as He rules and reigns at the end of the day. That is my dream. Is it yours?

Note

1 **Sammy Frye,** 2008; altered by **Dave Coats** 2012. Used with permission.

Day 5. Intimacy with God (4)

Daily Meditation Themes

- *Goodness of God:* "[Give] thanks to the Father, who has qualified you to share in the inheritance of the saints in light. He has delivered us from the domain of darkness and transferred us to the kingdom of his beloved Son, in whom we have redemption, the forgiveness of sins" (Col. 1:12–14).
- *Greatness of God:* "Bless the LORD, O my soul! O LORD my God, you are very great! You are clothed with splendor and majesty" (Ps. 104:1).

Song: "There is a Fountain Filled with Blood"

There is a fountain filled with blood
Drawn from Immanuel's veins;
And sinners plunged beneath that flood
Lose all their guilty stains.

The dying thief rejoiced to see
That fountain in his day;
And there may I, though vile as he,
Wash all my sins away.

Dear dying Lamb, Thy precious blood
Shall never lose its power,
Till all the ransomed church of God
Be saved, to sin no more.

E'er since, by faith, I saw the stream
Thy flowing wounds supply,
Redeeming love has been my theme,
And shall be till I die.[1]

Meditation

We have reached the fourth and last beautiful aspect of an intimate relationship:

List the five things you want to praise God most for. Now stop and think about what life would be like if you did not have these things. They are evidence of God's goodness to you.

_____
_____
_____
_____
_____
_____
_____
_____
_____
_____
_____

Small groups: What song of praise most expresses what you know and experience about God? Discuss it.

_____
_____
_____
_____
_____
_____
_____
_____
_____
_____
_____
_____
_____
_____

What do you expect out of life? What are your dreams, hopes, and treasures? Describe a life in which God is the focus, and explain how you see God at work in and around you through the events and situations you face. If your hopes and dreams do not revolve around God, where does He fit in your life?

———————————————
———————————————
———————————————
———————————————
———————————————
———————————————
———————————————
———————————————
———————————————

What would need to change in order for you to let God have control of your life? What fears do you need to put away?

———————————————
———————————————
———————————————
———————————————
———————————————
———————————————
———————————————
———————————————
———————————————
———————————————
———————————————
———————————————
———————————————
———————————————

WE WILL SHARE OUR THRILLS (LIFE EXPERIENCES)

When hard times come and great pressures come upon us, we are forced to rely on others and help one another stay the course. In the 1980s, my wife and I were in Haiti as missionaries. We were serving God and reaching souls for Christ. But the Lord took us through some very difficult times that included revolutionary crises, the near death of my wife, the kidnapping of one of our children, and my being put in jail by a crooked police system for a traffic accident. These events caused our relationship with and dependence on each other to be deepened.

As my wife lay in a medical facility with incompetent, third-world country staff, my concern for my wife was overwhelming. My dependence on God, however, was almost absolute. There was nothing else I could do but trust Him. The more we go through life in this kind of relationship with God, the more our depth of dependence and the reality of our trust will bear the fruit of a glorious and intimate relationship that will not go away.

Now that you understand meditation on God's Word, a deep relationship with God, and the power of the Word of God, you must find ways to develop that relationship biblically and direct it toward this kind of living. Since all Scripture is profitable for righteous, holy living, we know that some parts of Scripture most clearly lift our souls to God away from the cesspool and sewage of our culture. The Scriptures that most powerfully do that work are those directly focused on God, His goodness, and His greatness. Such passages point out to us and describe the God that we surely would enjoy giving our lives to.

Note
1 William Cowper, 1772.

Some of us may hear the concept of shared life experience and shrink back. I have shared some of the negative (from a human standpoint) from my life as a missionary. But I had to go through those experiences in order to also share in the positive and eternally rewarding experiences as well. Those positive experiences were also connected with the power and the presence of God. I am so thankful for them all. I know Him in a different way because He took me through those events.

I remember going back to Haiti in 2010 shortly after the devastating earthquakes that shook the country and its capital, Port-au-Prince. Because of what I had experienced in the 1980s in that country, I was able to do continuing ministry and to see incredible opportunities to share hope with these people. I saw God at work in the midst of death and destruction in ways I will never forget from those days in March and June of 2010.

Day 6. Focus on God in the Psalms: Praising Him for Who He Is and What He Does

God thoughts:

What moves you about God?

Daily Meditation Themes

- *Goodness and Greatness of God:* "He will wipe away every tear from their eyes, and death shall be no more, neither shall there be mourning, nor crying, nor pain anymore" (Rev. 21:4)

Song: "Face to Face"

Face to face with Christ, my Savior,
Face to face—what will it be?
When with rapture I behold Him,
Jesus Christ who died for me.

Face to face I shall behold Him,
Far beyond the starry sky;
Face to face in all His glory,
I shall see Him by and by!

What rejoicing in His presence,
When are banished grief and pain;
When the crooked ways are straightened,
And the dark things shall be plain.[1]

Meditation

Look for ways to come before the throne of God. Remember that the key to worship is the whole heart being engaged in praising and glorifying God (Ps. 86:12; 103:1).

- "I will be glad and exult in you; I will sing praise to your name, O Most High" (Ps. 9:2).
- "I will sing to the LORD, because he has dealt bountifully with me" (Ps. 13:6).
- "The LORD lives, and blessed be my rock, and exalted be the God of my salvation" (Ps. 18:46).
- "Surely goodness and mercy shall follow me

all the days of my life, and I shall dwell in the house of the LORD forever" (Ps. 23:6).

- "Remember your mercy, O LORD, and your steadfast love, for they have been from of old" (Ps. 25:6).
- "The LORD is my light and my salvation; whom shall I fear? The LORD is the stronghold of my life; of whom shall I be afraid?" (Ps. 27:1).
- "I believe that I shall look upon the goodness of the LORD in the land of the living!" (Ps. 27:13).
- "You have multiplied, O LORD my God, your wondrous deeds and your thoughts toward us; none can compare with you! I will proclaim and tell of them, yet they are more than can be told" (Ps. 40:5).
- "For the LORD, the Most High, is to be feared, a great king over all the earth" (Ps. 47:2).
- "Great is the LORD and greatly to be praised in the city of our God!" (Ps. 48:1).
- "Have mercy on me, O God, according to your steadfast love; according to your abundant mercy blot out my transgressions" (Ps. 51:1).
- "He will cover you with his pinions, and under his wings you will find refuge; his faithfulness is a shield and buckler" (Ps. 91:4).
- "Declare his glory among the nations, his marvelous works among all the peoples!" (Ps. 96:3)
- "For great is the LORD, and greatly to be praised; he is to be feared above all gods" (Ps. 96:4).
- "Praise him for his mighty deeds; praise him according to his excellent greatness!" (Ps. 150:2).

Note
1 **Carrie E. Breck,** 1898.

Small groups: Discuss what Revelation 21:4 expresses to us about God's power to put away all evil and pain. Also, discuss why God's goodness offers such hope to us. Paul uses the word "hope" to mean a confident expectation. Why is this hope, that death and pain will be done away with, possible?

A "biography of God" would be a list of things that God has done, will do, and what He is like. How would you put together a biography of God based on these verses from the Psalms?

Small groups: Share your "biographies" to encourage one another about what you see and have experienced of God.

_____
_____
_____
_____
_____
_____
_____
_____
_____
_____
_____
_____
_____
_____
_____
_____
_____
_____
_____
_____
_____
_____
_____
_____
_____
_____
_____
_____
_____
_____
_____
_____
_____
_____
_____

Day 7. Focus on the Cross

This week we finally come to the cross. It is a sight that should never entirely leave us. Perhaps we have become calloused to the image of the Son of God being nailed to the cross, crucified for us. We must remember that for a full six hours he hung there, exposed to the insults and hatred of the crowd and the shame of crucifixion. We shrink from pain. He had steadily driven Himself forward toward it.

He allows them to take the huge spikes and drive them through His hands and feet into the rough wood. He knows that this is the moment He must face on behalf of all fallen humankind. How else could Christ, the Son of God, die? Could He have died quickly? He must be sacrificed for humankind and bear the curse of the law. But Roman crucifixion is one of the most brutal and painful deaths a person can die. The spikes tear at Him, and His flesh becomes raw with the effort of pushing Himself up to get His breath. His lungs scream for oxygen that barely comes in fitful gasps.

Roman soldiers crucified Him, but they were simply carrying out the plan of God the Father. The Father was satisfied (Isa. 53:11) as He saw the anguish of His Son. In our Gospels the writers simply say, "And when they had crucified him …" (Matt. 27:35), or, "And they crucified him" (Mark 15:24): no long-drawn-out explanations. Can we draw the picture in our minds and on our hearts?

Daily Meditation Theme
- *Greatness of God:* "I will remember the deeds of the LORD; yes, I will remember your wonders of old. I will ponder all your work, and meditate on your mighty

Write out the impact on your heart of this visualization of the cross event.

_____
_____
_____
_____
_____
_____
_____
_____
_____
_____
_____
_____
_____
_____
_____
_____
_____
_____
_____
_____
_____
_____
_____
_____
_____
_____
_____
_____
_____
_____
_____
_____

deeds. Your way, O God, is holy. What god is great like our God? You are the God who
works wonders; you have made known your might among the peoples" (Ps. 77:11–14).

Song: "Hallelujah What a Savior"

"Man of Sorrows!" what a name
For the Son of God, who came
Ruined sinners to reclaim.
Hallelujah! What a Savior!

Bearing shame and scoffing rude,
In my place condemned He stood;
Sealed my pardon with His blood:
Hallelujah! What a Savior!

Guilty, vile, and helpless we;
Spotless Lamb of God was He;
Full atonement! Can it be?
Hallelujah! What a Savior!

Lifted up was He to die;
"It is finished," was His cry;
Now in heav'n exalted high.
Hallelujah! What a Savior!

When He comes, our glorious King,
All His ransomed home to bring,
Then anew this song we'll sing:
Hallelujah! What a Savior![1]

Note
1 **Philip P. Bliss,** 1875.

Week 6. Recognize What God Has Done

This week we will explore the ways that God's Word and His Spirit are changing you. Consider the words of the apostle Paul in Romans 8:28–29. He says, "And we know that all things work together for good, for those who are the called according to his purpose. For whom he foreknew he also predestined to be conformed to the image of his Son." What an amazing truth to know that God has a specific plan for my life. That plan is that I would be less and less like Dave Coats, the sinner. Instead, it is God's plan that I be more and more like Dave Coats the Christian, the follower and imitator of Christ. And through this study we are becoming CONFORMED to the likeness, the image, and the person of Christ. Rejoice!

Day 1. Recognize God's Work in Changing You

God thoughts:

Daily Meditation Themes

- *Goodness of God:* "God, being rich in mercy, because of the great love with which he loved us … made us alive together with Christ" (Eph. 2:4–5).
- *Greatness of God:* "There is none like you among the gods, O Lord, nor are there any works like yours" (Ps. 86:8).

Song: "How Sweet and Awesome"

How sweet and awesome is the place
With Christ within the doors,
While everlasting love displays
The choicest of her stores!

"Why was I made to hear Thy voice,
And enter while there's room,
When thousands make a wretched choice,
And rather starve than come?"

'Twas the same love that spread the feast,
That sweetly drew us in;
Else we had still refused to taste,
And perished in our sin.

Pity the nations, O our God!
Constrain the earth to come;
Send Thy victorious Word abroad,
And bring the strangers home.

We long to see Thy churches full,
That all the chosen race
May, with one voice, and heart, and soul,
Sing Thy redeeming grace.[1]

Meditation

Besides the church, the body of Christ, God has given us three main resources to help us change and become like Him. We have the Word, we have His Spirit, and we have His grace. We must expect that as we expose ourselves to the Word and allow it to find place in our hearts, God will change us. This is His plan. When others cannot help us, God will. When others are not with us, God is and so is His Word as we meditate on its truth.

Spend time over the next few days evaluating what God has done for you. Think back to what you were like when you started working through this book and began to address the struggle in your heart and life.

Small groups: Talk and share about God's work in these areas.

Spend time over the next few days evaluating what God has done for you. Think back to what you were like when you started working through this book and began to address the struggle in your heart and life.

1. Write down what you thought when you felt defeated.

_____
_____
_____
_____

2. What it was like to think that you might never overcome the sensual struggles of your mind?

_____
_____
_____
_____

3. Think about how often you fell in the beginning. At what point did you start seeing a difference? Why did this change happen then?

_____
_____
_____
_____

4. Which key Scriptures did God use to begin to renew your mind in regards to His power?

_____
_____
_____
_____

5. What has been your pattern of defeat—what day, time, and circumstances have generally been your downfall?

_____
_____

6. How has this pattern of defeat changed by God's grace?

7. Spend time in thanksgiving. Specifically, rejoice in the power of God that has changed you.

Note

1 Isaac Watts, 1707.

Day 2. The Breaking of Self and Its Will

Daily Meditation Themes

- *Goodness of God:* "[He has] raised us up with him and seated us with him in the heavenly places in Christ Jesus, so that in the coming ages he might show the immeasurable riches of his grace in kindness toward us in Christ Jesus" (Eph. 2:6–7).
- *Greatness of God:* "All the nations you have made shall come and worship before you, O Lord, and shall glorify your name" (Ps. 86:9).

Song: "God Be Merciful to Me"

God, be merciful to me,
On Thy grace I rest my plea;
Plenteous in compassion Thou,
Blot out my transgressions now;
Wash me, make me pure within,
Cleanse, O cleanse me from my sin.

My transgressions I confess,
Grief and guilt my soul oppress;
I have sinned against Thy grace,
And provoked Thee to Thy face;
I confess Thy judgment just,
Speechless, I Thy mercy trust.

I am evil, born in sin,
Thou desirest truth within;
Thou alone my Savior art,
Teach Thy wisdom to my heart;
Make me pure, Thy grace bestow,
Wash me whiter than the snow.

Broken, humbled to the dust
By Thy wrath and judgment just,
Let my contrite heart rejoice
And in gladness hear Thy voice;

God thoughts:

165

"Christ says 'Give me All. I don't want so much of your time and so much of your money and so much of your work: I want You. I have not come to torment your natural self, but to kill it. No half-measures are any good. I don't want to cut off a branch here and a branch there; I want to have the whole tree cut down. I don't want to drill a tooth, or crown it, or stop it, but to have it out. Hand over the whole natural self, all the desires which you think innocent as well as the ones you think wicked—the whole outfit. I will give you a new self instead. In fact, I will give you Myself: my own will shall become your own." (C. S. Lewis, *Mere Christianity*).[2]

How is your pride doing? Does humility have a lodging in your heart?

_____

_____

_____

_____

_____

Small groups: What will it take for you to humble yourself before the people around you? Has God changed you in this regard?

_____

_____

_____

_____

_____

From my sins O hide Thy face,
Blot them out in boundless grace.

Gracious God, my heart renew,
Make my spirit right and true;
Cast me not away from Thee,
Let Thy Spirit dwell in me;
Thy salvation's joy impart,
Steadfast make my willing heart.

Sinners then shall learn from me,
And return, O God, to Thee;
Savior, all my guilt remove,
And my tongue shall sing Thy love;
Touch my silent lips, O Lord,
And my mouth shall praise accord.[1]

Meditation

Let's go back to an idea that has been a main part of our discussion throughout this study. Self—and the effects of our drive for self-glory, self-protection, self-affection, self-pleasure, and other self-motives—is such a strong engine in the human condition that it must be broken. Pride is the arrogance of the human heart exalting itself against God. Meditate on the quotes below about pride. Absorb their truth in your heart. Analyze how you are doing in keeping a humble focus in your progress in purity.

- "But this is the one to whom I will look: he who is humble and contrite in spirit and trembles at my word" (Isa. 66:2).
- "Humility is honestly assessing ourselves in light of God's holiness and our sinfulness" (C. J. Mahaney[3]).
- "Pride is when sinful human beings aspire to the status and position of God" (C. J. Mahaney[4]).
- "God cannot bear with seeing his glory appropriated by the creature in even the smallest degree, so intolerable to him is

the sacrilegious arrogance of those who, by praising themselves, obscure his glory" (John Calvin[5]).

- "By the grace of God I am what I am, but God says absolutely, 'I am that I am'" (Matthew Henry[6]).

I have emphasized the need for daily meditation on the two themes of God's goodness and greatness. How powerful is this theme of God's greatness in your life? What difficulty do you have in believing it and sensing it with your whole heart? Consider that whenever you go through a day when you have not really taken time to meditate on God's greatness, you are tempted to be more in charge of your life, you are led to believe that your passions are under control, and you are more likely to become confident in yourself rather than dependent on God. If this is the case for you, it means that, in reality, *you don't believe what I am telling you.* You are not convinced that you must daily deny self and see yourself as *small* and God as *great.* You think the Christian life can be lived just in general acknowledgment of God, but not in a specific denial of your autonomy and His superiority. This will be your downfall. This has been my downfall in the past. We tend to drift in this direction. But it is so foolish. In fact, we never drift towards God. We must pursue Him to be like Him.

Notes

1 Richard Redhead, *The Psalter* (Pittsburgh, PA: The United Presbyterian Board of Publication, 1912), no. 140.

2 C. S. Lewis, *The Complete C. S. Lewis* (Signature Classics; New York: HarperSanFrancisco, 2002), 157.

3 *Humility: True Greatness* (Sisters, OR: Multnomah / Sovereign Grace Ministries, 2005), 22.

4 Ibid., 31.

5 Commentary on Psalm 9:1–3 in *Commentary on the Book of Psalms*, tr. **James Anderson** (Grand Rapids, MI: Eerdmans, 1963), n.p.

6 Commentary on Exodus 3 in *Matthew Henry's Concise Commentary on the Whole Bible* (Nashville: Nelson Reference, 2000), n.p.

Day 3. The Journey of Becoming Pure in Heart

God thoughts:

Daily Meditation Themes

- *Goodness of God*: "For by grace you have been saved through faith. And this is not your own doing; it is the gift of God, not a result of works, so that no one may boast" (Eph. 2:8–9).
- *Greatness of God:* "For you are great and do wondrous things; you alone are God" (Ps. 86:10).

Song: "Absent from Flesh"

Absent from flesh! O blissful thought!
What unknown joys this moment brings!
Freed from the mischiefs sin has brought,
From pains, and fears, and all their springs.

Absent from flesh! Illustrious day!
Surprising scene! Triumphant stroke!
That rends the prison of my clay;
And I can feel my fetters broke.

Absent from flesh! Then rise, my soul,
Where feet nor wings could never climb,
Beyond the heav'ns, where planets roll,
Measuring the cares and joys of time.

I go where God and glory shine,
His presence makes eternal day:
My all that's mortal I resign,
For angels wait and point my way.[1]

Meditation

Let's continue our discussion of how God is changing you. This should be a step of great encouragement to you at this point in your journey. Purity is a process: *a journey*. I hope you understand that. We don't suddenly become pure anymore than we can suddenly become "drug free." We do not suddenly, overnight, grow an oak tree of godliness from a sapling of worldly lusts. If your tendency is to focus on the times you fail or the times when your heart leans back toward the cesspool of sensuality, and it bothers you, this is excellent! Remember that in the past you weren't bothered much by those failures. Now you want to view the cesspool as disgusting and you want to be moved to pursue God more fervently. This is progress. Don't focus on any recent failures; focus on God's work in you. That is humbling. You see what only God can do.

God is at work. Thank Him for His work. Put a sign on your heart saying "Spiritual Work Zone." Notice your progress in the spiritual structure of your life. It is a tremendous thing to see this building work (Paul uses building terminology in 1 Cor. 3:9–10). See how the strengthening of your inner person will make your "building" a stronger one in Christ. Make a list of some of the new things God has brought into your life (we could call them "additions" to your building in Christ). The following words of George MacDonald, as quoted by C. S. Lewis, helps us understand why becoming pure as God is pure requires a major "renovation" of our inner being:

> Imagine yourself as a living house. God comes in to rebuild that house. At first, perhaps, you can understand what He is doing. He is getting the drains right and stopping the leak in the roof and so on: you knew that those jobs needed doing and so you are not surprised. But presently He starts knocking the house about in a way that hurts abominably and does not seem to make sense. What on earth is He up to? The explanation is that He is building quite a different house from the one you thought of—throwing out a new wing here, putting on an extra floor there ... You

Small groups: Discuss the progress you can see in one another since you have been meeting for encouragement in the growth of Christlikeness.

thought you were going to be made into a decent little cottage: but He is building a palace. He intends to come and live in it Himself.[2]

Notes

1 **Isaac Watts,** 1701–1709.
2 Quoted in **C. S. Lewis,** *Mere Christianity* (New York: Macmillan, 1943), 174.

Day 4. Failure and Growth (1)

Daily Meditation Themes

- *Goodness of God:* "You were at that time separated from Christ, alienated from the commonwealth of Israel and strangers to the covenants of promise, having no hope and without God in the world. But now in Christ Jesus you who once were far off have been brought near by the blood of Christ" (Eph. 2:12–13).
- *Greatness of God:* "Let the heavens praise your wonders, O Lord, your faithfulness in the assembly of the holy ones! For who in the skies can be compared to the Lord? Who among the heavenly beings is like the Lord?" (Ps. 89:5–6).

Song: "When Love Came Down to Earth"

When love came down to earth
And made His home with men,
The hopeless found a hope,
The sinner found a friend.
Not to the powerful
But to the poor He came,
And humble, hungry hearts
Were satisfied again.

What joy, what peace has come to us!
What hope, what help, what love!

When every unclean thought,
And every sinful deed,
Was scourged upon His back
And hammered through His feet.
The Innocent is cursed,
The guilty are released;
The punishment of God
On God has brought me peace.[1]

God thoughts:

171

Meditation

Today, we need to rehearse a part of your journey. We have spent a few days considering what God has done in your heart thus far. We have rejoiced in change. We must expect change. We must by faith believe what God says is on the way: a new person, someone progressively becoming entirely different from how he or she started out.

In fact, to settle for anything less is unbiblical. God created you in Christ Jesus for a new life (2 Cor. 5:17). But you may feel that there is more failure than growth and more struggle than victory. If so, note the following biblical observations.

First, remember that you must plan for daily victory and follow the biblical patterns for walking in the Spirit. If you give in to temptation, it is not because God forgot you. It is not because grace left you so that you had to wage war on your own (in the flesh) for a day. You did not somehow lose your ability to walk with God.

Sometimes people misquote Revelation 2:4 as "You have lost your first love." But notice that Christ does not say "lost" but "abandoned." These are two entirely different things. The first sounds like a mistake or that a bad thing happened to you. The second places the blame on you. It comes from a Greek verb that was used for a man who "put away" his wife. What a powerful image! Remember our discussion of the heart in Week 1. It is your heart desires and your own will that lead you either to walk in the Spirit or to fulfill the desires of the flesh.

Second, God's resources never fail. There has never been a day in history when God's supply was "not enough," and there never will be. God's promises and power are never limited or too small. His Word and his grace are "sufficient" so that God gets the glory in our weakness (2 Cor. 12:9). So do not get angry at

God or upset because of your latest struggle. God is sovereign and glorious. If you failed, it was because you just did not connect to His strength in your weakness. You failed to follow through with God's plan. Keep watching out for the ways your life allows openings that it should not allow for the flesh or the devil to enter in.

Note
1 **Stuart Townend** © 2001 Thankyou Music. EMI Christian Music Publishing.

Day 5. Failure and Growth (2)

Daily Meditation Themes

- *Goodness of God:* "… that he might … reconcile us both to God in one body through the cross, thereby killing the hostility … For through him we both have access in one Spirit to the Father" (Eph. 2:15–16, 18).
- *Greatness of God*: "Who … is like the Lord, a God greatly to be feared in the council of the holy ones, and awesome above all who are around him? O Lord God of hosts, who is mighty as you are, O Lord, with your faithfulness all around you?" (Ps. 89:6–8).

Song: "Speak, O Lord"

Speak, O Lord, as we come to You,
To receive the food of Your Holy Word.
Take Your truth, plant it deep in us;
Shape and fashion us in Your likeness.
That the light of Christ might be seen today
In our acts of love and our deeds of faith.
Speak, O Lord, and fulfill in us
All Your purposes for Your glory.

Teach us, Lord, full obedience,
Holy reverence, true humility;
Test our thoughts and our attitudes
In the radiance of Your purity.
Cause our faith to rise; cause our eyes to see
Your majestic love and authority.
Words of pow'r that can never fail—
Let their truth prevail over unbelief.

Speak, O Lord, and renew our minds;
Help us grasp the heights of Your plans for us—
Truths unchanged from the dawn of time
That will echo down through eternity.
And by grace we'll stand on Your promises,
And by faith we'll walk as You walk with us.

What is failure? Why do you find it so distasteful? Can God actually use failure as a motivation for godliness and a learning tool for good?

_____

_____

_____

_____

_____

_____

_____

_____

_____

_____

_____

_____

_____

_____

_____

_____

_____

_____

_____

_____

_____

_____

_____

Speak, O Lord, till Your church is built
And the earth is filled with Your glory.[1]

Meditation

We are remembering that failure and sin faults are never to be put to God's account. He has never let us down. We are to find the source of our return to impurity, slackness, a dry spiritual life, and other low times in our own hearts and their lack of commitment to meditation on God's ways. Perhaps you think I exaggerate the necessity of meditation. I could never do that. We so quickly tire of thinking godly thoughts and having a godly focus. We easily slacken in our pursuit of a pure mind and our longing for a holy heart. God does not.

Consider the following three verses and write out below how you can use them in your defense of purity:

- Romans 13:14: "Put on the Lord Jesus Christ, and make no provision for the flesh, to gratify its desires."
- Galatians 5:13: "Do not use your freedom as an opportunity for the flesh, but through love serve one another."
- Ephesians 4:27: "Give no opportunity to the devil."

The emphasis is on our choices. I am especially fascinated by the word "opportunity" in Galatians 5:13, the Greek word behind which can be used in a military sense to mean a "base of operations." So what are we doing to facilitate our flesh?

_____

_____

_____

_____

_____

Let's further address the issue of having an emotionally low day or a discouragingly poor week. Perhaps you even feel depressed. What of it? What can be done about this? We tend to allow our emotions to rule us and dominate what kind of a day or week we have. Instead, we need to inform our emotions through the truth we know. Meditating on God's goodness and greatness should inform our erratic emotions and help us do well in our battle with sensuality and its temptations. Our emotions are not to rule us; our thoughts and will are to move us in the right direction and our emotions and feelings must follow. Do not allow them to sidetrack you. Move through your emotions to higher ground in Christ Jesus.

Note
1 **Keith Getty and Stuart Townend** © 2005 Thankyou Music. EMI Christian Publishing.

Day 6. God's Grace at Work

Daily Meditation Themes

- *Goodness of God:* "So then you are no longer strangers and aliens, but you are fellow citizens with the saints and members of the household of God … in whom the whole structure, being joined together, grows into a holy temple in the Lord" (Eph. 2:19, 21).
- *Greatness of God:* "You rule the raging of the sea; when its waves rise, you still them … The heavens are yours; the earth also is yours; the world and all that is in it, you have founded them" (Ps. 89:9, 11).

Song: "Dearest Jesus"

Ah, dearest Jesus, how have You offended?
Man judges God, since You for us descended,
Coming to man's level bearing our affliction,
Facing man's derision, contempt, and rejection.

That man should judge his God, who was not guilty
'Twas sin's vile self, who brought this to Thee
Alas, my treason, Jesus, hath undone Thee.
'Twas I, Lord Jesus, who brought this on Thee!

Lo, the Good Shepherd for the sheep is offered.
The slave hath sinned, and the Son hath suffered;
For man's atonement, there alone Christ bleeds,
There our great and glorious God intercedes.

For me, kind Jesus, was Thy incarnation,
Thy mortal sorrow, and Thy life's oblation;
Thy death of anguish and Thy bitter passion,
For my great need was met in Thy salvation.

Therefore, kind Jesus, since I cannot pay Thee,
I do adore Thee, and will ever praise Thee,
Think on Thy pity and Thy love unswerving,
See Thy great passion for me undeserving.[1]

God thoughts:

Meditation

I mentioned earlier that we have four main resources given to us by God by which change and growth take place: the body of Christ, God's Word, His Spirit, and *grace*. Paul writes in 2 Corinthians 12:9, "But he [the Lord] said to me, 'My grace is sufficient for you, for my power is made perfect in weakness.' Therefore I will boast all the more gladly of my weaknesses, so that the power of Christ may rest upon me." Why did Paul need to take advantage of the grace God had given him? Because he was dealing with an ongoing struggle with some aspect of his life. God reminded Paul that he had what he needed to deal with this struggle.

Grace, then, is more than about salvation: it is also very much a part of our sanctification or growing in Christ. We can rejoice in our times of weakness that God makes us strong through His grace (see Paul's admonition to Timothy in 2 Tim. 2:1 that he is to be "strengthened by the grace that is in Christ Jesus"). Be encouraged that God has given you what you need to be satisfied in Christ today while you say "no" to the temptations of the world, the flesh, and the devil in the power of God's grace within.

Note

1 **Johann Heermann** (my revision of translation from German).

Day 7. Focus on the Cross

We must take a few moments to think further on what exactly took place at the cross. The big event can get lost in the physical pain of crucifixion. What was the big event? The reality and theological truth that Christ became sin for us. He who knew no sin (2 Cor. 5:21) became a curse for us (Gal. 3:13). There is no way we can understand this.

What did it mean for the God-Man, Christ Jesus? It meant that, although He was pure, He experienced impurity. Although He had never thought an evil thought, He knew evil in its most wicked forms. He had never once turned in rebellion from His Father, but now He saw all the rebellion of the human race against the kingdom of God from Adam to the present day. Such abominations and idolatrous horrors were brought upon God the Son at this moment for all humankind. How can we not weep as we see our own sins, rebellion, sensuality, pornography, idolatry, and other filth committed against a holy God placed on the shoulders of the Son?

Daily Meditation Theme
- *Greatness of God:* "You have a mighty arm; strong is your hand, high your right hand. Righteousness and justice are the foundation of your throne; steadfast love and faithfulness go before you" (Ps. 89:13, 14).

Song: "Here Is Love"

Here is love wide as the ocean
Loving kindness as a flood
When the Prince of Life, our ransom
Shed for us His precious blood
Who His love will not remember?

Cross thoughts:

179

Who can cease to sing His praise?
He can never be forgotten
Throughout Heaven's eternal days

On the mount of crucifixion
Fountains opened deep and wide
Through the floodgates of God's mercy
Flowed a vast and gracious tide
Grace and love like mighty rivers
Poured incessant from above
And Heaven's peace and perfect justice
Kissed a guilty world in love

Oh how marvelous, oh how glorious
Is my Savior's love for me!
Oh how marvelous, oh how glorious
Is my Savior's love for me!

Of Your fullness You are pouring
Your great love on me anew
Without measure, full and boundless
Drawing out my heart to You
You alone will be my glory
Nothing in the world I see
You have cleansed and sanctified me
You Yourself have set me free[1]

Note

1 Music and words by **Steve & Vikki Cook** © 2002 Sovereign Grace Worship (ASCAP). www.
SovereignGraceMusic.org. Used with permission.

Week 7. Encourage Yourself in God through His Word

The Word of God is filled with truth that we have not yet considered in this study on purity, because the study of purity is a study of our God. He is perfect purity and holiness. He is entirely different from us, but He wants us to be like Him. Make your study of God a study for life. As you study God, search always for truth that will change you into His image and likeness. Never be satisfied with any thoughts about God that cannot penetrate the deepest parts of your thinking and longings in life.

Psalm 119 will be the basis of our studying and enjoying God this week. The goal is to gain the insight and benefit that the psalmist did in his relationship to God through the Word.

Day 1. How Good Is God's Law for Us?

God thoughts:

Daily Meditation Themes

- *Goodness of God:* "Husbands, love your wives, as Christ loved the church and gave himself up for her, that he might sanctify her, having cleansed her by the washing of water with the word, so that he might present the church to himself in splendor, without spot or wrinkle or any such thing, that she might be holy and without blemish" (Eph. 5:25–27).
- *Greatness of God:* "Lord, you have been our dwelling place in all generations. Before the mountains were brought forth, or ever you had formed the earth and the world, from everlasting to everlasting you are God" (Ps. 90:1–2).

Song: "His Robes for Mine"

His robes for mine: O wonderful exchange!
Clothed in my sin, Christ suffered 'neath God's rage.
Draped in His righteousness, I'm justified.
In Christ I live, for in my place He died.

I cling to Christ, and marvel at the cost:
Jesus forsaken, God estranged from God.
Bought by such love, my life is not my own.
My praise—my all—shall be for Christ alone.

His robes for mine: what cause have I for dread?
God's daunting Law Christ mastered in my stead.
Faultless I stand with righteous works not mine,
Saved by my Lord's vicarious death and life.

His robes for mine: God's justice is appeased.
Jesus is crushed, and thus the Father's pleased.
Christ drank God's wrath on sin, then cried "'Tis done!"
Sin's wage is paid; propitiation won.

His robes for mine: such anguish none can know.
Christ, God's beloved, condemned as though His foe.
He, as though I, accursed and left alone;
I, as though He, embraced and welcomed home![1]

Meditation

Let's take time today to look at what God says about His Word and what we should do with it. Earlier, we considered the difference between meditating on and memorizing the Word. We will consider what the psalmist in Psalm 119 has to say about his relationship to the law.

Consider that when the psalmist referred to "the law" he was writing about the Torah. He was not writing about the words of Paul that are sweet to our souls, the Gospels that explain our salvation, or Peter's view of God in times of trouble. For the psalmist, the Law of Moses showed him a great and good God who was to be the focus of his heart and the joy of his inner man. Note what he says:

- verse 14: "In the way of your testimonies I delight as much as in all riches."
- verse 16: "I will delight in your statutes; I will not forget your word."
- verse 20: "My soul is consumed with longing for your rules at all times."
- verse 24: "Your testimonies are my delight; they are my counselors."
- verse 35: "Lead me in the path of your commandments, for I delight in it."

What is interesting to the student of this material is that the writer prefaces these words of love for the law with his reason for this love.

Notice verse 11. We get children and teens to memorize this verse to help them know that the Word of God is powerful and able to help them avoid sin. But there is a great depth of meaning in the Hebrew text. The psalmist says that he "has stored" the Word in his heart. The NASB translates this verb as "treasured." The Hebrew, *tsaphan*, means to lay up, to cherish,

Journal:

At this point in your journey toward a pure life, what can you see God doing in you and for you? What has changed so far in your heart? List a few things and share them with your small group if possible.

_____
_____
_____
_____
_____
_____
_____
_____
_____
_____
_____
_____
_____
_____
_____
_____
_____
_____
_____
_____
_____
_____
_____
_____
_____
_____
_____
_____
_____
_____
_____
_____
_____

to treasure. The writer of Proverbs uses this word when speaking of the wise man's care for knowledge. He "lays up" this knowledge for the sake of his life (Prov. 10:14).

So the writer of Psalm 119 is not saying to young people that they should simply memorize the law, but that, after memorizing it, they should cherish it, store it up, and treasure it as something dear to them. This is why he rejoices in, longs for, and delights in these testimonies of God.

Note

1 Chris Anderson. Copyright © 2012 Church Works Media. All rights reserved. Used by permission.

Day 2. How Does Our Joy in the Word Counsel Us Today?

Daily Meditation Themes

- *Goodness of God:* "For God so loved the world, that he gave his only Son, that whoever believes in him should not perish but have eternal life" (John 3:16).
- *Greatness of God:* "The LORD reigns; he is robed in majesty; the LORD is robed; he has put on strength as his belt. Yes, the world is established; it shall never be moved" (Ps. 93:1–2).

Song: "Come, Ye Sinners"

Come, ye sinners, poor and needy,
Weak and wounded, sick and sore;
Jesus ready stands to save you,
Full of pity, love and power.

I will arise and go to Jesus,
He will embrace me in His arms;
In the arms of my dear Savior,
O there are ten thousand charms.

Come, ye thirsty, come, and welcome,
God's free bounty glorify;
True belief and true repentance,
Every grace that brings you nigh.

Come, ye weary, heavy laden,
Lost and ruined by the fall;
If you tarry till you're better,
You will never come at all.

View Him prostrate in the garden;
On the ground your Maker lies.
On the bloody tree behold Him;
Sinner, will this not suffice?

God thoughts:

_____

So far you have been recording your thoughts in this workbook, but now is a good time for you to start a separate journal on the goodness and greatness of God. Keeping this kind of journal is a life-impacting activity that will be a blessing to you for years to come. Use your reflections on Psalm 119 as a starting point.

_____
_____
_____
_____
_____
_____
_____
_____
_____
_____
_____
_____
_____
_____
_____
_____
_____
_____
_____
_____
_____
_____
_____
_____
_____
_____
_____

Lo! th' incarnate God ascended,
Pleads the merit of His blood:
Venture on Him, venture wholly,
Let no other trust intrude.

Let not conscience make you linger,
Not of fitness fondly dream;
All the fitness He requireth
Is to feel your need of Him.[1]

Meditation

Reflect on the following meditations of the psalmist on the Word of God. As you do so, allow them to influence your attitude toward the Bible and your view of God through His Word. Then write down your thoughts about your own delight in God and His Word. How can your enjoyment of God through Scripture rival that of the psalmist?

- verse 40: "Behold, I long for your precepts."

_____
_____
_____

- verse 47: "I find my delight in your commandments, which I love."

_____
_____
_____

- verse 48: "I will lift up my hands toward your commandments, which I love, and I will meditate on your statutes."

_____
_____

- verse 70: "I delight in your law."

- verse 77: "Your law is my delight."

Note

1 **Joseph Hart,** 1759; refrain anonymous.

Day 3. How Sweet to Your Soul Is God's Law?

God thoughts:

Daily Meditation Themes
- *Goodness of God:* "For God did not send his Son into the world to condemn the world, but in order that the world might be saved through him" (John 3:17).
- *Greatness of God:* "Be still, and know that I am God. I will be exalted among the nations, I will be exalted in the earth!" (Ps. 46:10).

Song: "Grace Unmeasured"

Grace unmeasured, vast and free
That knew me from eternity
That called me out before my birth
To bring You glory on this earth.
Grace amazing, pure and deep
That saw me in my misery
That took my curse and owned my blame
So I could bear Your righteous name.

Grace (grace, grace)
Paid for my sins and brought me to life
Grace (grace, grace)
Clothes me with pow'r to do what is right
Grace (grace, grace)
Will lead me to heav'n where I'll see Your face
And never cease to thank You for Your grace.

Grace abounding, strong and true
That makes me long to be like You
That turns me from my selfish pride
To love the cross on which You died
Grace unending all my days
You'll give me strength to run this race
And when my years on earth are through
The praise will all belong to You[1]

Meditation
Continue to read through Psalm 119 and allow the richness of the psalmist's experience of

188

God through the Word to impact your view of the Word as well. Keep writing about the joy you can have in God through the rich treasure of His inexhaustible resources called the Scriptures. Let the psalmist influence you for good in this direction.

- verse 92: "If your law had not been my delight, I would have perished in my affliction."

  _____

  _____

  _____

  _____

- verse 97: "Oh how I love your law! It is my meditation all the day."

  _____

  _____

  _____

  _____

- verse 103: "How sweet are your words to my taste, sweeter than honey to my mouth!"

  _____

  _____

  _____

  _____

- verse 111: "Your testimonies are my heritage forever, for they are the joy of my heart."

  _____

  _____

  _____

  _____

- verse 113: "I love your law."

  _____

  _____

  _____

"From start to finish, the whole Christian life is by grace through faith. A new life in Christ commences with faith, continues by faith, and will be completed through faith. To put this another way, the Gospel is for Christians just as much as it is for non-Christians. We never advance beyond the good news of the cross and the empty tomb ... Therefore, the Christian always looks back to the Gospel and never to the law as the basis for his righteousness before God."[2]

_____

_____

_____

_____

_____

_____

_____

_____

_____

_____

_____

_____

_____

_____

_____

_____

_____

_____

_____

_____

_____

Notes

1 Music and words by **Bob Kauflin** © 2008 Sovereign Grace Praise (BMI). www. SovereignGraceMusic.org. Used with permission.

2 Philip Graham Ryken, *Galatians* (Reformed Expository Commentary; Phillipsburg, NJ: P&R, 2005), 90–92.

Day 4. Do You Love God's Law?

Daily Meditation Themes

- *Goodness of God:* "… looking to Jesus, the founder and perfecter of our faith, who for the joy that was set before him endured the cross, despising the shame, and is seated at the right hand of the throne of God" (Heb. 12:2).
- *Greatness of God:* "For we know him who said, 'Vengeance is mine; I will repay.' And again, 'The Lord will judge his people.' It is a fearful thing to fall into the hands of the living God" (Heb. 10:30–31).

Song: "Stand Up, Stand Up for Jesus"

Stand up, stand up for Jesus, ye soldiers of the cross;
Lift high His royal banner, it must not suffer loss.
From victory unto victory His army shall He lead,
Till every foe is vanquished, and Christ is Lord
    indeed.

Stand up, stand up for Jesus, stand in His strength
    alone;
The arm of flesh will fail you, ye dare not trust your
    own.
Put on the gospel armor, each piece put on with
    prayer;
Where duty calls or danger, be never wanting there.

Stand up, stand up for Jesus, the strife will not be
    long;
This day the noise of battle, the next the victor's song.
To those who vanquish evil a crown of life shall be;
They with the King of Glory shall reign eternally.[1]

Meditation

In our day, we often use words in ways that denigrate their meaning. "Love" is one such words. The psalmist describes his love for God's

Continue to build your "biography" and "works of God" journal here.

191

"Real importance is one thing, apparent importance another. The events which move the world are not always those which men think most noteworthy. The men who most deeply influence their fellows are not those of whom everybody is talking. The currents of thought and feeling which will shape the future are not those which are welcomed by the organs and interpreters of current opinion. When Christ appeared, the palace of the Caesar seemed to be more likely to govern the destinies of mankind than the manger of Bethlehem. No, brethren, depend on it, the apparent is not always, or even generally, the real."[2]

Word by picturing the Scriptures as something to be prized and enjoyed above anything else that this world values. As you continue to absorb the psalmist's thoughts, write out your own reflections on how God's Word is becoming something you value highly because it brings a great and good God to you.

• verse 119: "I love your testimonies."

_____

_____

_____

• verse 127: "I love your commandments above gold."

_____

_____

_____

• verse 140: "Your promise is well tried, and your servant loves it."

_____

_____

_____

• verse 143: "Your commandments are my delight."

_____

_____

_____

• verse 159: "Consider how I love your precepts!"

_____

_____

_____

Notes

1 **George Duffield, Jr.,** 1858. Public domain.

2 **H. P. Liddon,** *Christmastide at St Paul's* (London: Longmans, Green and Co., 1889), 101–102.

Day 5. Do You Long to Spend Time in the Word?

God thoughts:

Daily Meditation Themes

- *Goodness of God:* "Now may the God of peace who brought again from the dead our Lord Jesus, the great shepherd of the sheep, by the blood of the eternal covenant, equip you ..." (Heb. 13:20–21).
- *Greatness of God:* "'God opposes the proud, but gives grace to the humble.' Submit yourselves therefore to God. Draw near to God, and he will draw near to you ... Humble yourselves before the Lord, and he will exalt you" (James 4:6–8, 10).

Song: "O The Deep, Deep Love"

O the deep, deep love of Jesus,
Vast, unmeasured, boundless, free!
Rolling as a mighty ocean
In its fullness over me!
Underneath me, all around me,
Is the current of Thy love;
Leading onward, leading homeward
To Thy glorious rest above!

O the deep, deep love of Jesus,
Spread His praise from shore to shore!
How He loveth, ever loveth,
Changeth never, nevermore!
How He watches o'er His loved ones,
Died to call them all His own;
How for them He intercedeth,
Watching o'er them from the throne!

O the deep, deep love of Jesus,
Love of ev'ry love the best!
'Tis an ocean vast of blessing,
'Tis a haven sweet of rest!
O the deep, deep love of Jesus!
'Tis a heav'n of heav'ns to me;

194

And it lifts me up to glory,
For it lifts me up to Thee.[1]

Meditation

Consider how the Word of God is the basis of our salvation. What joy and delight does this bring to us? As you work through the following verses, reflect on how easy it is to take our salvation, our God, and His Word for granted. We can treat them lightly. Write about your own battle against apathy and think how the time you spend in the Word that brings you your Savior should be a remedy for this apathy.

- verse 162: "I rejoice at your word like one who finds great spoil."

_____
_____
_____
_____
_____

- verse 163: "I hate and abhor falsehood, but I love your law."

_____
_____
_____
_____
_____

- verse 167: "My soul keeps your testimonies; I love them exceedingly."

_____
_____
_____
_____
_____

- verse 174: "I long for your salvation, O LORD, and your law is my delight."

"The meaning of all misery in the world is that sin is horrific. All natural evil is a statement about the horror of moral evil. If you see a suffering in the world that is unspeakably horrible, let it make you shudder at how unspeakably horrible sin is against an infinitely holy God. The meaning of futility and the meaning of corruption and the meaning of our groaning is that sin—falling short of the glory of God—is ghastly, hideous, repulsive beyond imagination. Unless you have some sense of the infinite holiness of God and the unspeakable outrage of sin against this God, you will inevitably see the futility and suffering of the universe as an overreaction. But in fact the point of our miseries, our futility, our corruption, our groaning is to teach us the horror of sin. And the preciousness of redemption and hope."[2]

_____
_____
_____
_____
_____
_____
_____
_____
_____

Notes

1 **Samuel Trevor Franci**s (1834–1925).

2 **John Piper,** message entitled "Subjected to Futility in Hope, Part 1," April 28, 2002, available at http://www.desiringgod.org/resource-library/sermons/subjected-to-futility-in-hope-part-1; accessed July 2012.

Day 6. What Have You Learned about God and His Word?

Daily Meditation Themes

- *Goodness of God:* "Blessed be the God and Father of our Lord Jesus Christ! According to his great mercy, he has caused us to be born again to a living hope through the resurrection of Jesus Christ from the dead, to an inheritance that is imperishable, undefiled, and unfading, kept in heaven for you" (1 Peter 1:3–4).
- *Greatness of God:* "[We] by God's power are being guarded through faith for a salvation ready to be revealed in the last time" (1 Peter 1:5).

Song: "All I Have Is Christ"

I once was lost in darkest night
Yet thought I knew the way
The sin that promised joy and life
Had led me to the grave
I had no hope that You would own
A rebel to Your will
And if You had not loved me first
I would refuse you still.

But as I ran my hell-bound race
Indifferent to the cost
You looked upon my helpless state
And led me to the cross
And I beheld God's love displayed
You suffered in my place
You bore the wrath reserved for me
Now all I know is grace.

Hallelujah! All I have is Christ
Hallelujah! Jesus is my life.

God thoughts:

God thoughts:

Now, Lord, I would be Yours alone
And live so all might see
The strength to follow Your commands
Could never come from me
Oh Father, use my ransomed life
In any way you choose
And let my song forever be
My only boast is You.[1]

Meditation

So the psalmist has a deep love for the Word and he has cultivated a longing in his soul to experience more of the reality of God through the law, God's revelation of Himself to His people. Take a few moments to reread the comments you have written down this week and then see if you can bring them together into a sentence or two to express your long-term relationship with God through His Word.

Part of the core change that I am helping you develop is a habit of studying God's Word daily for yourself. You cannot feed your spiritual life arbitrarily, sometimes studying it for yourself and other times just going to church to hear what others know about God. Yes, you must read the Bible to be nurtured toward spiritual growth.[2] But this general feeding of your spiritual life as you read through the Bible is not enough to conquer the effects of impurity of the heart and defilement of the passions! When it comes to gaining victory over the flesh and the lusts you have infected your soul with, you must find specific biblical truth that will attack the cheap stuff you have allowed to touch your inner being.

Sometimes we get caught up in the *form* of Christian activities (such as reading or praying) and lose the joy of the relationship side. Then we tend to avoid "doing" these things because they have become a type of formalism and have lost their reality. But what we need to do is to move from the *duty* to the *delight* in our walk with God. Don't stop spending time in the Word or in prayer (and Ps. 119 is, after all, the psalmist's prayer to God) just because you feel these have become stale, formal activities. Address your heart longings and passions. Reorient them toward a good and great God. That is what the psalmist is expressing to us. Consider these thoughts:

- You must find verses and passages that key in to the renewal of your mind. These verses must focus on God and not man.
- You must understand 2 Corinthians 7:9–11 (see Week 1) , which will help you stay on course for victory. Godly sorrow or repentance must be a vital part of the renewing of your mind.
- You must meditate on God's glory, beauty, holiness, and majesty. Such thoughts are the opposite of lustful man-centered thoughts. Passages such as Isaiah 6 and Revelation 4–5 provide a view of God that does not allow for the pleasure of self and the sewage of the mind.

So:

- Understand what has happened in the deepest part of your soul. You have been infected by a deadly, sensual virus that causes you to lust for satisfaction in the cheap, bawdy, and twisted pleasures of the flesh. You allowed this to happen by choice. You had a temporary thrill that awakened gross and sinful desires for enjoyment in shameful activities or images.
- Unfortunately, you had no idea how deeply this quick thrill would touch you. But that is how God made you. The arena of sex is so pure but also so private that it should be enjoyed within your home with your soul-mate and no one else. When

Explain the impact of a selfish, sensual act on a person's family, ministry, and life. Why do you think this does not stop more people from falling into sexual sin?

_____

If a pastor or theologian can fall into sexual sin, are you or I exempt from this temptation?

_____

What must be in place in order for us to avoid such a fall?

_____

What is the greatest experience you have known or seen that really left an impact on you?

_____

you allowed yourself a cheap imitation of this, it touched you deeply but left you unsatisfied, wanting more.

- More importantly, it is at this level of intimacy that we are to enjoy and worship God. Many of us have never known what it is to have a relationship with God at our deepest level of being, but that is what He has designed us to do. We are to worship Him and be affected deeply by the reality of His presence and His being.
- In order to attack this "virus" that we have allowed to penetrate our being, we must use the "intravenous" drip of *truth* to penetrate our souls as well. A few minutes of prayer and a brief devotional thought will not remove the soul infection we have contracted.
- We must learn how to meditate on God's glory, majesty, and beauty, so that these realities thrill us far more than a cheap sin-flick. We must be moved and desire the glory of God and the awesome nature of His character above this world's imitation and replacements. Then, when the cheap world picture shows up, we will hate it and see it for what it really is: disgusting, revolting, and contemptible.

Consider what John Piper says,

> My conviction is that one of the main reasons the world and the church are awash in lust and pornography (by both men and women—30 percent of Internet pornography is now viewed by women) is that our lives are intellectually and emotionally disconnected from the infinite, soul-staggering grandeur for which we were made. Inside and outside the church Western culture is drowning in a sea of triviality, pettiness, banality, and silliness. Television is trivial. Radio is trivial … Education is trivial. Christian books are trivial. Worship styles are trivial. It is inevitable that the human heart, which was made to be staggered with the supremacy of Christ, but instead is drowning in a sea of banal entertainment, will reach for the best natural buzz that life can give: sex … The deepest cure is to be intellectually and emotionally staggered by the infinite, everlasting, unchanging supremacy of Christ in all things.[3]

We are totally missing that for which we were designed. Our finding satisfaction in things so much less grand than God is disgusting and sad. But how will we change this pattern unless we learn to meditate on *Him*? Take time to write down some of what you have learned about meditating on God and how you can enjoy this. See what the psalmist says in Psalm 36:8: that those who find a place of rest in Christ will feast on the "abundance" of His house, and will drink from the "river of [His] delights." Now that is a great picture.

_____

_____

_____

_____

_____

_____

_____

_____

Notes

1 Music and words by **Jordan Kauflin** © 2008 Sovereign Grace Praise (BMI). www. SovereignGraceMusic.org. Used with permission.

2 Remember the CCPP model I mentioned in Day 2 of Week 5 that can help you in your personal Bible study: reflect on *God's Commands*, *God's Character*, *God's People*, and *God's Promises*. Make your study of Scripture a study of God. Get to know Him. Experience the reality of God in your life by faith. An example of such a study can be found in Appendix 2.

3 John Piper, "Sex and the Supremacy of Christ: Part Two," in **John Piper and Justin Taylor,** (eds.), *Sex and the Supremacy of Christ* (Wheaton, IL: Crossway, 2005), 44; available online at http://www.desiringgod.org.

Day 7. Focus on the Cross

God thoughts: He was forsaken so that we would never be alone.

Today we want to consider the words Jesus cried out on the cross: "My God, my God, why have you forsaken me?" (Matt. 27:46). This fulfillment of prophecy (Ps. 22:1) represents one of the deepest truths and greatest mysteries of our Bible. We cannot begin to imagine this act of God the Judge toward God the Son. Nor can we explain it. What we do believe is that this event was part of what the Son saw was ahead of Him when he prayed in the Garden. He was emotionally burdened by the sense of loneliness this thought brought. Jesus took on Himself the sins of the whole world. God "made [Jesus] to be sin" (2 Cor. 5:21) for us: he took the "hit" for us.

We cannot imagine having a perfect relationship with someone. But we know what it is like when we are enjoying a good relationship on the human level and then one single sin enters in and breaks the communion, fellowship, and unity of our friendship. We quickly feel the change in the relationship.

Imagine a whole truckload of sin, iniquity, and wretched behavior being put to our name in that situation. We would be flabbergasted. We would be emotionally hurt, pained, and broken by the loss of the unity and by the emptiness we would feel. Now add to that the fact that the iniquity is not our own but instead is *assumed* to be ours. In addition, we must bear this burden and not stand up for our own name.

So the Son of God takes the brunt of our guilt and shame, burden and pain for sin, including the loss of fellowship with His Father. All creation is in darkness and seemingly broken over this event. Silence and emptiness hang over the scene and nothing can be resolved until the blood is spilt and the sin debt is paid. When Christ cries out "It is finished," He is not only letting us know that redemption is complete, but also that His pain and separation from the Father have come to an end. To God be the glory!

Daily Meditation Theme

- *Greatness of God:* "For we know him who said, 'Vengeance is mine; I will repay.' And again, 'The Lord will judge his people.' It is a fearful thing to fall into the hands of the living God" (Heb. 10:30–31).

Song: "Creation Sings the Father's Song"

Creation sings the Father's song;
He calls the sun to wake the dawn
And run the course of day
Till evening falls in crimson rays.
His fingerprints in flakes of snow,
His breath upon this spinning globe,
He charts the eagle's flight;
Commands the newborn baby's cry.

Hallelujah! Let all creation stand and sing,
"Hallelujah!" Fill the earth with songs of worship;
Tell the wonders of creation's King.

Creation gazed upon His face;
The ageless One in time's embrace
Unveiled the Father's plan
Of reconciling God and man.
A second Adam walked the earth,
Whose blameless life would break the curse,
Whose death would set us free
To live with Him eternally.

Creation longs for His return,
When Christ shall reign upon the earth;
The bitter wars that rage
Are birth pains of a coming age.

Cross thoughts:

When He renews the land and sky,
All heaven will sing and earth reply
With one resplendent theme:
The glories of our God and King![1]

Note

1 Words and Music by **Keith and Kristyn Getty and Stuart Townend** © 2008 Thankyou Music. EMI Christian Publishing.

Week 8. Answer the Key Question

As we come to Week 8 you must answer a very important question: How are you doing? What has happened in your life during these last seven weeks? Has there been change? We have looked at the possibility that you might have hit a "spiritual speed bump" along the way that has slowed you down and perhaps caused you discouragement. That kind of failure or setback is normal, and it is not a cause for concern unless it sends you all the way back to the starting line again. That would not be good.

When you look back over the last weeks, how would you describe them? Revolutionary, or a continual battle with no end in sight? Would you say that you are seeing more victory than failure? Would you say that the waves of temptation are not as strong as they used to be, and that your desire for God has blossomed? Most importantly, do you find anything inside you that drives you forward and motivates you in your heart to keep trying? Or is this a seemingly fruitless exercise in spiritual disciplines and activity that makes no real sense to you? Do the daily meditation times seem pointless? Do you fail to enjoy the time with God and in praise of Him? Are you wondering why God does not take away from you your lust and drive toward the cesspool of sensuality?

If you have spent seven weeks in this study and are no closer to a more victorious, passionate walk with God, then one of two things is true. Either your view of sanctification is wrong and this study has not changed that, or you don't have the power of God in your life at all; He is not within your heart and life to change you. That possibility is what we will look at this week.

Day 1. Are You a Child of God?

Daily Meditation Themes

- *Goodness and Greatness of God:* "… In hope of eternal life, which God, who never lies, promised before the ages began and at the proper time manifested in his word through the preaching with which I have been entrusted by the command of God our Savior" (Titus 1:2–3)

Song: "My Jesus, Fair"

My Jesus, fair, was pierced by thorns,
By thorns grown from the fall.
Thus He who gave the curse was torn
To end that curse for all.

O love divine, O matchless grace—
That God should die for men!
With joyful grief I lift my praise,
Abhorring all my sin,
Adoring only Him.

My Jesus, meek, was scorned by men,
By men in blasphemy.
"Father, forgive their senseless sin!"
He prayed, for them, for me.

My Jesus, kind, was torn by nails,
By nails of cruel men.
And to His cross, as grace prevailed,
God pinned my wretched sin.

My Jesus, pure, was crushed by God,
By God, in judgment just.
The Father grieved, yet turned His rod
On Christ, made sin for us.

My Jesus, strong, shall come to reign,
To reign in majesty.
The Lamb arose, and death is slain.
Lord, come in victory![1]

Meditation

Today's meditation will either be a tremendous blessing to you or something that drives you to the greatest battle of your life. Are you really a child of God? *That is the key question.* Are you born of God—born again? Have you come from darkness into light? This week's studies will either confirm that your heart is the dwelling place of the Son of God and His Spirit, or strongly suggest that you are lost.

Ask God right now to make this matter clear to you. Remember that the Bible says you are either a child of God or a child of the devil. You are either lost or saved. You have either been born again or you are dead in sin. There is no in-between state; there is no middle ground when it comes to salvation. If you are relying on a prayer you prayed once for God to save you, or some other "assurance" prayer, you were misled. It means you are not sure whether you are lost or saved.

Let me be perfectly clear. I am dealing with this issue during the last week of our study because pornography is not the unpardonable sin. Many children of God have fallen into pornography's trap. It is a huge, alluring, cesspool of sensuality. That is not the real problem I am addressing. You can be saved and fall into any sin. But why does pornography dominate you and beat you? Why do you not see victory in your life? You have all the resources you will ever need, and you have been given the understanding to use them. So what is missing? If this is your situation, maybe—probably—you are not a true, genuine child of God. You can argue with God, not with me, about that. So I will give you God's Word, His explanation, of what you should be like as a child of God.

In Appendix 8 you will find the testimonies of two men who battled pornography for years and finally came to the realization that they had nothing to fight it with. They had no biblical motivation—only the motivations of fear and self-preservation. They had nothing of God's power in their lives. The testimony of R below is similar:

> I prayed a prayer to be saved at age six but because of moral issues started doubting my salvation as a teen. I spent the next six years doubting and fearing whether I was lost or saved. I looked at my prayer and asked, Is it good enough? Now I am eighteen and every time I start thinking about whether my salvation is real or not I get all tight inside. Fear grips me. What do I do? I don't think I can believe now or have the faith to pray. It seems useless.

My response to R and to anyone else in his position is this: It is not about your prayer. It is about God. Either you are saved or you are lost. You should fear being lost and not dealing with it. There is no in-between state (praying a "prayer of assurance" just clouds the issue). You need to see what God says in His Word: does He say you are saved? If He does not show you that there is fruit of real regeneration (that you are born again), you must resolve that. Faith is the other side of repentance. You cannot truly turn from your sin and to God in salvation until you know you are lost.

Note

1 Chris Anderson. © Copyright 2008 churchworksmedia.com. All rights reserved. Used by permission.

Day 2. Do You Have the Spirit Within?

Daily Meditation Themes

- *Goodness and Greatness of God:* "Now to him who is able to keep you from stumbling and to present you blameless before the presence of his glory with great joy, to the only God, our Savior, through Jesus Christ our Lord, be glory, majesty, dominion, and authority, before all time and now and forever" (Jude 24–25).

Song: "Jesus, Thank You"

The mystery of the cross I cannot comprehend
The agonies of Calvary
You the perfect Holy One crushed Your Son
Who drank the bitter cup reserved for me

Your blood has washed away my sin
Jesus, thank you
The Father's wrath completely satisfied
Jesus, thank you
Once Your enemy, now seated at Your table
Jesus, thank you

By Your perfect sacrifice I've been brought near
Your enemy You've made Your friend
Pouring out the riches of Your glorious grace
Your mercy and Your kindness know no end.[1]

Meditation

In 1 Corinthians 2:14 Paul says that the "natural person does not accept the things of the Spirit of God." In the Bible, the fool is the person who rejects what God says and what the Bible teaches. Why do unsaved fools do this? Because they do not have the Spirit of God within them to help them desire the good things of God. They do not understand why they would want to follow God, because it is a spiritual choice encouraged by the Spirit within. *It blows my*

God thoughts:

Small groups: Discuss what this chapter in Romans is saying about a person with God's Spirit within. Share the reality with one another.

_____

mind in studying Matthew 1–3 what went on here. The evidence is overwhelming that Jesus is the promised Messiah. Yet the teachers of the OT rejected Him. Why? They are blind to truth. They do not know God. As in Matthew 1-3, today, people grow up around the Bible, even memorize the Bible, but it has no effect on them. Why? They do not know God. They do not have the Spirit to open their eyes to see truth. They are unchanged.

Read the following verses from Romans 8:

- 8:9: "Anyone who does not have the Spirit of Christ does not belong to him."
- 8:14: "For all who are led by the Spirit of God are sons of God."
- 8:16: "The Spirit himself bears witness with our spirit that we are children of God."

How do you know that the Spirit is within you today?

Note

1 2003 Sovereign Grace Worship. Integrity's Hosanna! Music. EMI Christian Music Publishing.

Day 3. Does God Lovingly Correct You?

Daily Meditation Themes

- *Goodness and Greatness of God:* "I am the Alpha and the Omega, the beginning and the end. To the thirsty I will give from the spring of the water of life without payment" (Rev. 21:6).

Song: "Your Holy Majesty"

You are high above all things
The heavens can't contain
Your radiance and Your beauty
You shine brighter than the sun
I'm ravished and undone
You've conquered me completely
Now I am longing for the time
When I will see Your …

Holy, holy majesty
Your glory and Your splendor
Holy, holy majesty
You fill my soul with wonder
And unspeakable delight
At just the sight
Of Your holy majesty

Why would You shed Your own blood
For those who spurned Your love
And so many times refused Your grace
Why would You take up our curse
Why did You love us first
Oh You deserve eternal praise
Now I am longing for the time
When I will see Your …[1]

Meditation

Read Hebrews 12:5–12. Every true child of God will bear the marks of God's chastisement. *Because God loves His children* He will use different levels of correction, admonition, and "whipping" to bring them to Himself.

If I can live contrary to God's Word and in disobedience to His commands without any evidence of God's correction, I am in trouble. The fruit of God's chastisement is righteousness. So as you look at your life up to this point, is it

Small groups: Do you understand how God's love and chastening are connected and not antithetical? Also, do you understand the difference between when God punishes evil and when He lovingly corrects His children?

characterized by God's work in your heart and His regular, loving pursuit of you in your sin? When you have messed up in sin, do you see God at work, or does He seem to be removed from you?

Note

1 **Mark Altrogge,** 2001, Sovereign Grace Praise (BMI). EMI Christian Music Publishing.

Day 4. Is Your Faith Dead or Alive?

Daily Meditation Themes

- *Goodness and Greatness of God:* "No longer will there be anything accursed, but the throne of God and of the Lamb will be in it, and his servants will worship him … And night will be no more. They will need no light of lamp or sun, for the Lord God will be their light, and they will reign forever and ever" (Rev. 22:3, 5).

Song: "I Stand in Awe'"

You are beautiful beyond description
Too marvelous for words
Too wonderful for comprehension
Like nothing ever seen or heard
Who can grasp Your infinite wisdom
Who can fathom the depths of Your love
You are beautiful beyond description
Majesty, enthroned above

And I stand, I stand in awe of You
I stand, I stand in awe of You
Holy God, to whom all praise is due
I stand in awe of You.

You are beautiful beyond description
Yet God crushed You for my sin
In agony and deep affliction
Cut off that I might enter in
Who can grasp such tender compassion
Who can fathom this mercy so free
You are beautiful beyond description
Lamb of God, who died for me[1]

Meditation

James 2:17–18 says, "Faith by itself, if it does not have works, is dead … Show me your faith apart from your works, and I will show you my faith by my works." James is not speaking of

213

Small groups: Does everyone in the group understand James's point here? He is not supporting works salvation.

being justified before God but being justified before people. The evidence (or justification) of what we say is confirmed by how we live. Living faith is evident to people around us. They can tell that our faith is at work in our lives.

On the other hand, those who only *claim* to have faith are like the demons who have a mental assent to God's existence and power but are not changed. Their lives deny their words about their faith.

Note

1 Music and words by **Mark Altrogge** © 1986 Sovereign Grace Praise (BMI). www. SovereignGraceMusic.org. Used with permission.

Day 5. Are You Born of God and in the Light?

Daily Meditation Themes

- *Goodness and Greatness of God:* "...
  Waiting for our blessed hope, the
  appearing of the glory of our great God
  and Savior Jesus Christ, who gave himself
  for us to redeem us from all lawlessness
  and to purify for himself a people for his
  own possession who are zealous for good
  works" (Titus 2:13–14).

Song: "God of Grace"

God of grace, amazing wonder,
Irresistible and free.
Oh, the miracle of mercy;
Jesus reaches down to me.
God of grace, I stand in wonder
As my God restores my soul;
His own blood has paid my ransom;
Awesome cost to make me whole.

God of grace, who loved and knew me
Long before the world began;
Sent my Savior down from heaven;
Perfect God and perfect man.
God of grace, I trust in Jesus,
I'm accepted as His own;
Every day new grace sustains me
As I lean on Him alone.

God of grace, I stand astounded,
Cleansed, forgiven and secure.
All my fears are now confounded
And my hope is ever sure.
God of grace, now crowned in glory,
Where one day I'll see Your face;
And forever I'll adore You
In Your everlasting grace.[1]

God thoughts:

Meditation

Today we will study 1 John and note the places where the text identifies what the true children of God are like:

- 2:9–11 "is still in darkness": The text makes it clear that hatred of anyone who is a Christian is not compatible with being in the light. Such a person is still in darkness, a metaphor for being without God. This is explained in 3:15, where John says that hatred is like murder and that "no murderer has eternal life." Your attitude toward Christians is a key to what is really in your heart.

- 2:29 "born of Him": Who is described in this way? Someone who "practices righteousness." If we practice righteousness, when we look at our lives we will see right choices, righteous desires, righteous ways. We are not perfect, but regularly living right as a pattern.

- 3:9–10—those who are "born of God" and "children of God" are made evident by their lifestyles and practices, as also seen in 2:29. John intends us to compare our overall direction and life patterns with what God says should be true. If we are children of God, we will be practicing right living and choices on a regular basis. If we do not do this, God will bring correction and chastening so that we will come back to the right path and direction. We know when God is pursuing us.

- 3:14 "we love the brothers": we love the Christians in our community, our church, and our part of the world. We desire to be with them and be a part of what they do and pursue with them what they are pursuing. Our hearts enjoy their company and their life direction.

Note

1 **Jonathan Rea and Keith Getty,** 2003 Thankyou Music. EMI Christian Music Publishing.

Day 6. Is There Evidence That God Lives in You?

Daily Meditation Themes

- *Goodness and Greatness of God:* "But when the goodness and loving kindness of God our Savior appeared, he saved us, not because of works done by us in righteousness, but according to his own mercy" (Titus 3:4–5).

Song: "I Will Sing of My Redeemer"

I will sing of my Redeemer
And His wondrous love to me;
On the cruel cross He suffered,
From the curse to set me free.

Sing, oh sing, of my Redeemer,
With His blood He purchased me,
On the cross, He sealed my pardon,
Paid the debt, and made me free.

I will tell the wondrous story,
How my lost estate to save,
In His boundless love and mercy,
He the ransom freely gave.

I will praise my dear Redeemer,
His triumphant pow'r I'll tell,
How the victory He giveth
Over sin, and death, and hell.

I will sing of my Redeemer,
And His heav'nly love to me;
He from death to life hath brought me,
Son of God with Him to be.[1]

Meditation

Continuing in 1 John, reflect on the following:

- 3:24 "he abides in us": we know that if we have God within us, His Spirit is present to help us know that He is within. The Spirit works with the Word of God to give us a confidence in God's work in our lives. In other words, He changes us so that we will want to obey God and keep His commandments/Word. Without this, we would be unable to live the way God asks us to. A living person always shows evidence of life, and this

Small groups: With the help of your leader, encapsulate John's thoughts into a couple of sentences.

_____
_____
_____
_____
_____
_____
_____
_____
_____
_____
_____
_____
_____
_____
_____
_____
_____
_____
_____
_____
_____
_____
_____
_____
_____
_____
_____
_____
_____
_____
_____

is especially true of spiritual life. Those who have no spiritual life within yet pretend to be believers will eventually realize that they are fooling themselves and others. They are making artificial attempts at life, but God is not within them to help them. So looking at your life overall, do you have evidence of God's life within you, of His Spirit working in you?

- 5:1 "Everyone who believes that Jesus is the Christ has been born of God": some people read this verse and say that "believe" means giving mental assent. However, the word "believe" in the Bible pictures a confidence and assurance which shows up in the way a person lives. So a believer is one who does not merely assent to the mental truth that Jesus exists, but lives in such a way that he or she _demonstrates_ that Jesus is the promised Messiah (another name for the Christ). For members of the early New Testament church who believed that Jesus had fulfilled the promises of the Messiah, His life, miracles, death, and resurrection became the center of their lives. Their belief influenced their behavior and drove their obedience. This was why they became known as _Christians_ (Christ followers, Christ disciples).

- 5:4 "overcomes the world": What does it look like to overcome the world? And what does it look like to _be overcome by_ the world? John says in the second half of this verse that faith is the victory that overcomes the world, the system opposed to God. Do I believe that God will help me live for Him, and that He already does this? Am I overcome by the world? Do I regularly fall to the world system and give in to its pressures and appeals? Is my life generally characterized by spiritual failure and sinful living like the world around me, or is it characterized by spiritual living that reflects God? Again, as you look back on your life thus far, is it characterized more by a worldly philosophy and the things that this world promotes and lives for, or is it characterized by God's ways? Is there evidence of living by faith, or of living by sight and what you see in this world?

Note

1 **Philip P. Bliss,** 1876.

Day 7. Focus on the Cross

Cross thoughts:

Consider the people hanging on crosses on either side of Jesus. Split over their response to Jesus, the Son of God, they represent, in a sense, the two sides of history. Both are on the precipice of eternity. Both have the opportunity to turn to Jesus for rescue—but only one does so. The other disdains the very Savior of the world who is dying for this condemned criminal's wicked acts. What a picture of us all! Christ must die so that we have hope when we face death. He conquers death so that we don't have to fear it. Jesus hangs on the tree, bearing our sin, so that our sin can be removed. The one criminal pleads in faith for God's mercy, while the other rejects the mercy hanging next to him. Here on the cross, the greatness and goodness of God are in full view. Only a good God would offer to take on the sins of condemned criminals, and only a great God could take those sins and remove them as far as the east is from the west.

Daily Meditation Theme
- *Greatness of God:* "It is finished" (John 19:30).

Song:"I Cannot Tell"

I cannot tell why He whom angels worship
Should set His love upon the sons of men,
Or why, as shepherd, He should seek the wanderers,
To bring them back, they know not how or when.
But this I know, that He was born of Mary,
When Bethlehem's manger was His only home,
And that He lived at Nazareth and labored,
And so the Savior, Savior of the world is come.

I cannot tell why Christ the Father's only Son
In garden lonely bowed His sacred head;

The ground stained dark with blood-like sweat from
    holy brow;
The cup of sin He took there in my stead.
But this I know: the soldiers led the Son of God
To walk the street to face the hate-filled ones;
They spit upon the holy, sinless, Lamb of God,
Then led Him forth to crucify God's only Son.

I cannot tell why all the hosts of heaven
Watched silently this seeming sad defeat;
The mocking words, the crown of thorns that pierced His brow,
The tearing flesh, the nail-pierced hands and feet.
But this I know: that God the Father turned away;
He could not bear the sin-clad form below;
There all alone, on Calvary's hill, Christ bore our sin;
He bowed His head and conquered our great foe.

I cannot tell how silently He suffered,
As with His peace He graced this place of tears,
Or how His heart upon the cross was broken,
The crown of pain to three and thirty years.
But this I know, He heals the brokenhearted,
And stays our sin, and calms our lurking fear,
And lifts the burden from the heavy laden,
For yet the Savior, Savior of the world is here.

I cannot tell how He will win the nations,
How He will claim His earthly heritage,
How satisfy the needs and aspirations
Of east and west, of sinner and of sage.
But this I know, all flesh shall see His glory,
And He shall reap the harvest He has sown,
And some glad day His sun shall shine in splendor
When He the Savior, Savior of the world is known.

I cannot tell how all the lands shall worship,
When, at His bidding, every storm is stilled,
Or who can say how great the jubilation
When all the hearts of men with love are filled.
But this I know, the skies will thrill with rapture,
And myriad, myriad human voices sing,

And earth to heaven, and heaven to earth, will answer:
At last the Savior, Savior of the world is king![1]

I think we need to try to put into words the impact and the importance of these words: "It is finished." Consider personally that God was at that very moment accepting the work and the life of Jesus as sufficient for my sin and for my failure to live up to God's standard. Consider historically that God was in the midst of finishing what He began in eternity for mankind. God's words, "It is finished," reflect His pattern throughout history. What He says, He will do. DONE.

Note

1 Vv. 1, 4, 5, and 6 by **William Young Fullerton** (1857–1932); vv. 2 and 3 by **Dave Coats.**

Appendix 1.

Accountability in the Battle for Purity

A life pattern of accountability could be a means for your help and encouragement in the battle for the purity of your soul. You will at times feel lonely and perhaps exposed to the sensual darts of the one who would destroy your soul, family, and ministry. You need a friend who will encourage and admonish you.

Some hear the word "accountability" and assume it is a form of "Gestapo" Christianity that looks over your shoulder. Yet from the Bible we see that there needs to be a sense of mutual discipleship and care for one another. In order for you to see the biblical nature of accountability, I recommend that you take time to do a study of the "one another" passages in the New Testament. We are to love one another, encourage one another, build one another up, speak good to one another, submit to one another, comfort one another, pray for one another, bear one another's burdens, admonish one another, and so on.[1] We cannot do any of these things intelligently and intensively unless we regularly spend one-on-one time with other believers.[2]

- For your accountability, choose someone you can be totally honest with and you know will check up on you.
- Find a time each week when you can meet to talk, review Scripture truth, and find encouragement.
- Plan to pray together for at least ten minutes over the issues of life that help you, stretch you, and build you.
- Especially plan time to worship God together in prayer (and song if possible).

Your counselor or accountability partner could ask the following questions on a regular basis:

1. What were your weak times of temptation this week?
2. What specific thoughts and actions did you allow (masturbation, viewing pornography, etc.)?
3. What was the exterior source of these thoughts? Did something you were exposed to bring them up?
4. Were you too casual in your guard against immoral input?
5. When do you struggle the most with wrong thoughts? (Are there certain times of the day? Are there certain situations? When are you the most open to temptation?)
6. How did you respond to these thoughts? Did you fight them or did you get more involved?
7. Have you repented of these thoughts? Do you see them as the Bible describes sin? Do you recognize your thoughts as being as sinful as the immoral acts they lead to?

8. Have you been honest about this with those who are close to you?
9. Which of the following are problems for you: TV, DVDs, electronic games, phone usage, music, Internet, e-mail chat rooms, certain stores, or certain areas in specific stores?
10. Can I check your laptop? Does it have images on it that serve your sensuality?
11. Do you need to disconnect your cell phone Internet service?
12. Are you being faithful about replacing wrong thoughts with those that focus on God and which view men/women correctly? Are you memorizing Scripture to help this process? Are you daily focused on the goodness, beauty, holiness, majesty, and glory of God? Were you faithful this week in reviewing these truths?
13. Do you need to take drastic measures ("Put to death …," Col. 3:5) or do radical amputation of a spiritual nature? This might mean removing the TV, not going into the DVD rental stores, disconnecting the Internet (or locking yourself out from it so that only other family members can use it), or avoiding the stores and places that are a temptation for you. Do you need to have others check up on you frequently for a period of time?
14. Have you been faithful in your Bible reading and prayer life? Do you daily commit this battle to God and call on His help? When you have sensed temptation coming, did you call out to God for His help?
15. Do you find encouragement from the following list?
    • God has already overcome this struggle for you in Christ (Rom. 6).
    • You have His promise of grace in times of testing (2 Cor. 12:9).
    • You know that God will not test you above what you can bear (1 Cor. 10:13).
    • God will always love you no matter what (Rom. 8:35–39).
    • God wants you to be godly like Him, being conformed to the image of Christ (Rom. 8:29).
    • God will never leave you (Matt. 28:20).
    Remember:
    • Be thankful for God's patience, grace, and goodness.
    • Don't be proud or you will fall. Always consider your weakness and God's strength.
    • Never feel sorry for yourself. Allow the goodness of God to bring you to repentance.
    • Do not blame others or your situation for your fall.
    • Keep your goal in mind: to be a godly version of yourself.
    • When temptation comes (1 Tim. 6:11–12):
        • Flee the lusts: run!
        • Fight the devil: take the battle to him!
        • Follow Christ: have a purpose and goal that drive you in the right direction!

Notes

1 1 Thes. 5:11; Gal. 5:15, 26; James 4:11; 1 Thes. 4:18; Rom. 12:10; Gal. 5:13; Heb. 10:24; Eph. 5:21; Rom. 15:7; James 5:16; Gal. 6:2, 5; Eph. 4:32; Rom. 15:14; Col. 3:16; Rom. 13:8.

2 It can also be profitable to have an accountability group—perhaps three or four men or women who meet weekly to encourage one another. This group can pray, study, and worship God together in ways that will build their mutual love and care for a holy walk with God.

Appendix 2. Personal Bible Study Example

Passage: Philippians 1
God's commands: (none found)
God's character: God shows us what He is and what He does
- v. 2—God is the source of grace and peace
- v. 6—God is doing a work in us until we see Christ
- v. 19—God the Spirit helps us in our times of difficulty

God's people: God gives us believers who model godliness for us
- v. 1—Paul is a servant, not a high and mighty leader
- v. 3—Paul is an example of godly concern and prayer
- v. 7—Paul has a heart relationship with these believers
- v. 8—Paul loves these people dearly
- vv. 9–10—Paul's prayer includes concern for their spiritual growth in knowledge, discernment, and fruit to God's glory
- vv. 12–13—Paul's adverse circumstances do not keep him from sharing the gospel; in fact, he uses the circumstances as a gospel platform
- vv. 20–21—In life or death, Paul's focus is not self, but God and His glory

God's promises: God gives us His Word to cling to
- v. 6—God is not finished with us; He will work in us

Meditation/Application for My Life

1. I need God's grace. I will fail without it. I must daily ask Him for this supernatural strength to live for Him. God wants me to have His grace; why would I ignore it? How can I be so arrogant as to live apart from God's grace? Thank you, God, for grace—your grace, daily grace, sufficient grace. I live in a world that lacks peace. People struggle and cause strife because of their pride. What about me? Is peace possible in my life? Can the peace of God be a daily reality in my walk?

2. I am amazed at what God is doing in me. If I did not know of, or could not see, anything God had done in my life recently, I would wonder if He was at work in me at all. I want to see His hand at work in my life. Life seems short when I consider what God must do in my heart to change me into His likeness and image. Thank You, God, for being patient with me and working with me.

3. I don't consider the Spirit's work often enough. What a great life companion He is! In fact, He is at work when I struggle most and when I have the greatest need. Thank You, God, for Your Spirit, the gift of life He gave me, and the work of holiness He is doing in me.

4. I don't live like Paul. I am too convinced of my leadership abilities and "stuff." It is really hard for me to be a servant. I want to be like Christ in this way. I need to be

humbled daily before God, knowing what I owe Him and what He has done for me. God, break me of self and help me to be a servant.

5. I am too self-focused and not concerned about others. I need this model of others' concern. I do not pray enough for those around me. I don't even know all their needs. How can I pray like this for them and bring them to God? God, help me see others' needs and speak to You on their behalf.

6. God, please develop in me a love for others, as You have loved them. Let me not be judgmental or particular in choosing those whom I help and involve myself with.

7. Paul had a unique ability to turn life's "lemons" into lemon juice. He saw God's hand and work through the turmoil and trouble of his own life. God, help me to see You in every part of my life and ministry.

8. God, may I never quit until I see You. You will not quit on me until You see me.

Appendix 3. Further Meditation Themes

1. Below I have listed a few "targeted prayer" verses from Romans, along with some personalized responses. Study them, consider their implications for yourself, and use them to help develop a thankful heart. Then follow the same format for other verses you find in the Scriptures. Small-group leaders can use these passages to become a source of blessing in their group's focus on God. Build your own group notebook, including a biography of God and a record of your thankfulness to Him.

God's wrath is coming	Romans 2:5 (But I will never face God's wrath—hallelujah!)
God's glory is too high for me to meet it	Romans 3:23 (But He has shared His glory and in Christ made it possible for me to overcome the deep rift between God and my sinful soul.)
I didn't seek God	Romans 3:11 (But God in His goodness sought me as a sinner, lost, condemned, and not knowing my need of Him.)
Christ died for me	Romans 5:8 (Thank God! This is God's goodness and His greatness. Only God could satisfy His wrath.)
Sin requires the death penalty	Romans 6:23 (But God was good enough to pay that penalty for me.)
Whoever calls on the name of the Lord will be saved	Romans 10:13 (But I would not have called on Him unless I had heard the word that God in His goodness sent to my family, and unless He opened my heart to His message.)

2. Consider whole passages in Scripture, rather than single verses, that focus on God's work in bringing the gospel, salvation, and its blessings to your life.

These passages will probably be great meditation themes for both the "goodness" and the "greatness" of God. For example, in Romans 1:16 I am reminded that I am indebted to God for His good work of bringing the message of the cross to my life. God did not owe me that work. He put me in a home where I would hear the gospel. God is *good*! But I also recognize that it is the power of God, His *greatness* as Sovereign of the universe, that causes this to be true. Not only that, but it is His spiritual power in the gospel of the cross that broke my heart over my sin. What a great God! What power!

Other examples are Ephesians 1:3–14, an incredible passage, as well as 1 Peter 1:3–5.

3. Consider passages that focus on God's creation, His power, His authority, and His transcendence.

4. Read the meditations of godly people throughout time who have helped us understand the work of God in our redemption and the work of the cross. Here are some examples:

I find no balm for a sore conscience, and a troubled heart, like the sight of Jesus dying for me on the accursed tree. There I see that a full payment has been made for all my enormous debts. The curse of that law which I have broken has come down on One who there suffered in my stead. The demands of that law are all satisfied. Payment has been made for me, even to the uttermost farthing. It will not be required twice over. Ah! I might sometimes imagine I was too bad to be forgiven. My own heart sometimes whispers that I am too wicked to be saved. But I know in my better moments this is all my foolish unbelief. I read an answer to my doubts in the blood shed on Calvary. I feel sure that there is a way to heaven for the very vilest of men, when I look at the cross (J.C. Ryle).[1]

In the stupendous matter of our salvation Christ shall be the Alpha and the Omega. With Him the gospel plan originated—by Him it was revealed—by Him it was executed—and in His undivided glory and endless praise it shall forever terminate. From every tongue in glory, and through the high arches of heaven, the anthem shall peal, "Worthy is the Lamb!" Believer in Christ! Does not your soul pant to join in that song? and does not your spirit exult in the truth that salvation, from first to last, is of God? Oh, how precious is this truth in the consciousness of our many failures and defects! Our salvation is all in Christ—our righteousness is all in Christ—our merit is all in Christ—our completeness is all in Christ—in Christ our Covenant Head, our Surety and Mediator; and no flaw in our obedience, no defect in our love, no failure in our service, should so cast us down as to shut our eye to our acceptance in the Beloved. Imperfections we would not overlook, sin we would not allow, disobedience we would not indulge, temptation we would not encourage; nevertheless, we would ever remember, for our encouragement that, in default of perfection in the most perfect of our own doings, we are fully and eternally complete in Jesus (Octavius Winslow).[2]

The Cross of Christ is certainly a noble example of self-sacrifice; but if it be only a noble example of self-sacrifice, it has no comfort for burdened souls; it certainly shows how God hates sin; but if it does nothing but show how God hates sin, it only deepens our despair; it certainly exhibits the love of God, but if it does nothing but exhibit the love of God it is a mere meaningless exhibition which seems unworthy of God. Many things are taught us by the Cross; but the other things are taught us only if the really central meaning is preserved, the central meaning upon which all the rest depends. On the cross the penalty of our sins was paid; it is as though we ourselves had died in fulfillment of the just curse of the law; the handwriting of ordinances that was against us was wiped out; and henceforth we have an entirely new life in the full favor of God (J. Gresham Machen).[3]

5. Use the *names* of God as meditation starters for your day: Almighty God, Alpha and Omega, Ancient of Days, Bread of Life, Christ Jesus my Lord, Wonderful Counselor, Creator, Desire of All Nations, Father of Mercies, Everlasting Father,

Great God and Savior, God of Hosts, God Most High, God of Glory, God of Heaven
and Earth, God of My Salvation, God the King, King of Kings, Lord of Lords, High
Priest, Eternal Spirit, Holy God, The Great I AM, Immanuel, Jesus the Christ, Judge
of All the Earth, King of Glory, God of Gods, Living God, King of the Jews, Man
of Sorrows, Mediator of the New Covenant, Messiah, Christ Our Passover, Great
Physician.

Notes

1 "The Answer to My Doubts," quoted at "Of First Importance," http://firstimportance.org/,
April 2, 2010; accessed June 2012. This Web site is a marvelous resource that can send you a daily
e-mail quote for your encouragement.

2 "Alpha and Omega," quoted at "Of First Importance," http://firstimportance.org/, September
16, 2007; accessed June 2012.

3 "The Central Meaning of the Cross," quoted at "Of First Importance," http://firstimportance.
org/, September 21, 2007; accessed June 2012.

Appendix 4. Starter Journal

Text: _____   Date: _____

Thoughts: _____

_____

_____

_____

_____

_____

_____

_____

_____

_____

Personal Application (How I Should Live Out the Word): ___

_____

_____

_____

_____

_____

_____

_____

_____

_____

_____

_____

_____

_____

_____

_____

_____

(*continued*)

Appendix 5. The Struggle with Masturbation

Note: I have tried to keep most of this study guide as exempt from explicit sexual references as possible up to this point. But I cannot handle this topic without being clear. Read this section with care and only when you are definitely in the situation already and in need of help and counsel.

Masturbation is an activity that is not usually addressed during teen Bible classes or adult Bible studies, yet it is prevalent, perhaps even prolific, among youth groups and older men and women. This is a topic we need to address in this workbook, for at least three reasons. First, masturbation often accompanies other areas of purity struggles. Second, this struggle affects both men and women. Third, and finally, we have spoken of the need to reset the conscience (Week 1), but if the topic of masturbation is not addressed, the conscience will not be properly set.[1]

As you journey through life, it will quickly become apparent that there is a diversity of opinion when it comes to the application of biblical principles to real life. This is especially true when it infringes on areas of a person's private life that he or she has guarded for some time. People may admit that certain public actions, such as displays of pornographic material, are wrong, but they may not see their own private activities and pleasures as evil.

Surveys show that roughly 75 percent of guys who come into Bible college have had some level of struggle with pornography or purity of mind and body. This may have been a struggle that was brief or it may be a battle that has been ongoing for months and even years. Rarely have

Is masturbation something that all believers should be encouraged to do so that it becomes the norm? Why or why not?

_____

_____

_____

We should do all things for God's glory and His honor (1 Cor. 10:31). How does this apply to masturbation?

_____

_____

_____

The body is God's temple. We are not our own (1 Cor. 6:19–20). Apply how this truth relates to masturbation.

_____

_____

_____

We must discern what is pleasing to the Lord (Eph. 5:10). Do not say that others must prove what is wrong with masturbation; you must prove beyond doubt that it is right.

_____

_____

_____

_____

they been honest enough to lift the veil on their inner battle, much less to get serious discipleship help.

Pornography and all other means of stirring up lusts of the heart cry out for release and fulfillment of some kind. Masturbation gives a man or woman this release and temporary fulfillment. But with the initial fulfillment comes a demand for more. Since the man or woman cannot have a sexual partner now, he or she feels that masturbation is the next best thing.

How does this activity start? Usually, it is at the time when young people first experience body changes that show they are now adult men and women that they have their first physical reactions to sensual images. By the way, God designed us to become adults at a certain age. Our emotional and intellectual maturity must keep step with our physical maturity. We must not treat womanhood and manhood as something that comes with the age when we can vote or drink.

For men, it is important to distinguish between a "wet dream" and masturbation. A deep-sleep dream that moves your body to respond physically is not masturbation. You are in subconscious mode and your body is simply responding to the stimuli given it by your brain images. As a young adult man, you are becoming aware of the opposite sex and drawn to it. Masturbation, on the other hand, takes place during conscious, waking hours. I must be direct: some people have learned to manipulate their morning times into fantasy worlds of sensuality. What I mean by this is that you can wake up and then allow yourself to drift between waking and sleeping, but you know that you want the images and desires to come back so that you can experience your physical sex drive.

A man may dream or fantasize about his dream woman, probably with a body that he can picture from something he has seen. While fantasizing this way, he then enjoys the sexual experience alone. Some will simply act out the selfish sex act to get over their physical drive that seems out of control. Their lust drives and controls them. They worship their sexual feelings.

For the woman, since she cannot find someone who will pursue her, desire her, and want her body, she may begin masturbating in order to find temporary satisfaction. She will solace herself in the fact that she can do without a man if necessary. She will go on the Internet and get the visual stimulation she may need. She may even go to same-sex sites. Since men don't find her attractive, she may decide she was not destined to be attractive to them, so perhaps her attraction will be found among women. The married woman may feel rejected or used only for a temporary need by her husband. She must deal with this by looking to God.

People will give many *unbiblical reasons* why masturbation should be allowed:

- This activity is God's way of helping men and women make the journey to marriage without committing adultery or fornication.
- This act will help men and women avoid having an affair if they are not satisfied sexually with their spouses.
- It can help mates who are away from their spouses for some time.

- Masturbation relieves depression and helps self-worth.
- It seems there is no scientific evidence to show this act to be harmful to the body.
- Guilt about masturbation is self-imposed or driven by judgmental Christians.
- "Good" Christians differ on this subject, so we shouldn't get too worried about it.
- As long as you are not lusting while doing masturbation, it is OK. We just shouldn't let masturbation get out of control.

Some are convinced that masturbation cannot be overcome and nor should it be. They may suggest that fighting masturbation will only drive it behind closed doors. Nothing works as a "cure." This leaves the young adult who does not find a life mate in college wondering what he or she should do. Do adults "burn," as Paul says in 1 Corinthians 7:9? Will this sex drive slowly go away if appeased by masturbation?

From experience, I know that teens who begin to use masturbation as a means of escape and pleasure become young adults who continue in this pattern—only they are not satisfied with what got them through their teen years. Why? Because masturbation is only a temporary fix, a bridge to more exciting sexual pleasures. Remember that Jesus, a single man, said that we must deny self, take up our cross, and follow Him (Luke 9:23). He did not say, "Allow yourselves enough pleasure in order to make it through the temptations you face. Allow yourselves some fulfillment of the desires and passions that at times drive your body." You will not be convinced by my "opinions" on this subject, so study it for yourself. You will have to give account to God for what is done in your body.

1. Study *porneia*, the Greek word that we translate as "fornication." In biblical times this word covered a wide range of sexual

Write down your thoughts about what you are reading. This is necessary in order to let the full impact of the cross event sink into your heart. If helpful, write out a prayer of thanks to God which includes the specifics of what the Son of God did there. If you can continue your self-sex and self-pleasure acts at the foot of the cross, with the holy Son of God looking down from it, then continue on.

Masturbation and self-sex: now that we have brought the topic out into the open, we must be committed to biblical thinking in this area. If you struggle with this, explain why you do it. What is its purpose? Is it godly or self-driven?

_____

_____

_____

_____

Explain when and how you do it. Does this seem like behavior that is godly? Why do you hide?

_____

_____

_____

_____

If this is harmless and there is no wrong in it, it is just like drinking a can of pop. You can stop whenever you want to. Is this true?

_____

_____

_____

_____

Can you stop doing it? Does it have control over you physically, emotionally, spiritually?

_____

_____

_____

activities both outside and inside marriage. The translation "immorality" is a good fit for this word. Moulton and Milligan's study of the vocabulary of the Greek New Testament points out that originally this word meant "prostitution." Eventually, it applied to all kinds of general sexual activity.[2] The *porne* in the Greek was a prostitute or harlot.

2. Paul says in 1 Corinthians 7:1–5 that in order to avoid *porneia*, the husband and wife are to give each other their "conjugal rights."[3] So if one or the other partner desires sex, it is not to be withheld. The inference is that when sex is withheld from a partner, he or she tends to seek some form of satisfaction outside the bounds of the marriage relationship. The problem, Paul says in verse 5, is a lack of self-control. However, if one of the marriage partners is being self-centered, he or she will want only what he or she feels to be his or her *right*. Yet 1 Corinthians 13:4–7 pictures a love that is totally unselfish. Write down how this passage affects your struggle with masturbation.

3. The following are practical helps in overcoming the addiction to self-sex pleasure.

• See yourself as an "addict." I know—you don't see yourself in that way. But don't forget that sin by its very nature is addictive. It gives the pleasure of sin for a time and makes you want to keep going back for more. So see yourself that way. One man in my office used to struggle with addiction to cigarettes, pornography, and alcohol, and I asked him how he viewed his masturbation compared with these others. He saw the alcohol and so on as addictions he had to conquer, but not masturbation. Just because an addiction is more private or hidden, that does not make it less life-controlling. This hidden sin still violates God's moral law and holiness just as much as if you were stealing from a child to feed your cocaine addiction. It breaks God's standard of righteousness just as much as abusing your spouse because of alcohol addiction.

- Understand the *rituals* (patterns) of the addict. As addicts to sin, we have routines or rituals that lead us down the path toward the pleasure of the act of masturbation. What are they? What are you thinking at these times? On what days and at what times are you most likely to give in to this pleasure? What do you feel and desire at this point? Why don't you see God's presence and His displeasure? Do you do it after a long day of work? Do you think you deserve something for self after sacrificing all day long? Do you think your body is your own, to do with as you please? What are you thinking that you need?

- See how you worship pleasure more than you worship God at this point. Put this sign over that path to pleasure: "There is a way that seems right to a man, but its end is the way to death" (Prov. 14:12). You might excuse it as OK, but it will destroy you. If you give in to this on your bed or at the shower, commit yourself instead to getting down on your knees and talking to God at those times, rather than getting into your self-pleasure drive. You have set up this thrill on the altar of your heart as something you believe you must have or must do. That is a lie to self.

- Change your thinking so that you find total satisfaction in Christ. We must not excuse masturbation because, for example, of the actions of our mate. The husband who blames lack of satisfaction in his relationship with his wife for his need to masturbate is still seeking sexual satisfaction outside the marriage bed. Sex within marriage is the only design God made.

- "Cry out to God Most High" (Ps. 57:2[4]) when the wave of temptation to masturbate comes. If you're in bed, get out. Fall on your face before God. Then, if it helps, go and get some exercise. Fast if you must. Fasting is a great spiritual exercise for the one who struggles with the lusts of the flesh. Why? Because God commands us to deny ourselves and find our satisfaction in Christ alone. So when you deny yourself food for a time and give yourself instead to the spiritual pleasure of prayer in worship of God, you are sacrificing the flesh and choosing to walk in the Spirit. It will help, I promise. But your heart must be fixed. You must plan this out ahead of time. Now that you know your ritual worship of self-pleasure, you must plan to worship God and find satisfaction in Him alone, while you are alone. Remember it is when you are alone that you give in to the secrecy of your addiction. So here in your closet of prayer, all alone with God, fasting and praying, you can finally know the joy of loving and worshiping only God.

Notes

1 If you are a leader of a small group, I suggest you set aside some time to work through this topic. For some, opening up about it will not be easy. Lead the way. Ask if someone can share generally what battle he or she faces with the body. Offer to talk to people privately about this struggle. This may pave the way for others to open up.

2 *Porneia* in **James Hope Moulton and George Milligan,** *The Vocabulary of the Greek New Testament* (Grand Rapids, MI: Eerdmans, 1985), 529.

3 He teaches them that their sex drives and sexuality do not exist for their own self-satisfaction. Instead, when we come to know Christ, we are given the self-sacrificing love of God (*agapé*) which seeks the benefit of another instead of self. Thus the focus of our sexuality is our mate first, not self. I exist for my wife, not for my own sexuality. *Agapé* love exists to give and fulfill the other; my satisfaction is a byproduct. This does not suggest that I do not want sex. It says that I must put aside my drive and selfishness and think first of my partner (Phil. 2:3–4). Some teach that men have greater sex needs than women, but the Bible does not support this. If my wife cannot "meet my needs," does that mean I can then go and find sex satisfaction elsewhere? God forbid. If she becomes an invalid, what then? If she is pregnant, am I to allow my drive for sex to dominate the relationship? *Agapé* will not.

4 If you believe you cannot beat this addiction, get your study Bible, concordance, or online Bible and study in the Psalms how many times the psalmist "cried out" to God. Notice the contexts in which the psalmist was desperate. He found himself at the end of any human means of salvation from trouble. You may be in that place too.

Appendix 6.
Questions That Expose Our Hearts[1]

1. What do you love? Hate?
2. What do you want, desire, crave, lust, and wish for?
3. What do you seek, aim for, pursue? What are your goals and expectations? What are your plans, agendas, strategies, and intentions designed to accomplish?
4. Where do you bank your hopes?
5. What do you fear? What do you not want? What do you tend to worry about?
6. What do you feel like doing?
7. What do you think you need?
8. What makes you tick? What sun does your planet revolve around? Where do you find your garden of delight? What lights up your world? What really matters to you? Around what do you organize your life?
9. Where do you find refuge, safety, comfort, escape, pleasure, security?
10. What or whom do you trust?
11. Whose performance matters? On whose shoulders does the well-being of your world rest? Who can make it better, make it work, make it safe, make it successful?
12. Whom must you please? Whose opinion of you counts? From whom do you desire approval and fear rejection? Whose value system do you measure yourself against? In whose eyes are you living? Whose love and approval do you need?
13. Who are your role models? What kind of person do you think you ought to be or want to be?
14. On your deathbed, what would sum up your life as worthwhile? What gives your life meaning?
15. How do you define and weigh success or failure, right or wrong, desirable or undesirable, in any particular situation?
16. What would bring you the greatest *pleasure*, happiness, and delight? The greatest pain and misery?
17. Whose victory or success would make your life happy? How do you define victory and success?
18. What do you want to get out of life? What payoff do you seek out of the things you do? "What do you get out of doing that?"
19. What do you think about most often? What preoccupies or obsesses you? In the morning, to what does your mind drift instinctively? What is your "mindset"?
20. What do you talk about? What is important to you? What attitudes do you communicate?
21. How do you spend your time? What are your priorities?
22. What are your characteristic fantasies, either pleasurable or fearful? Daydreams?

23. How do you live for yourself?
24. Where do you find your identity? How do you define who you are?

Note

1 Taken from "Seeing with New Eyes" by **David Powlison** ISBN 978–0-87552–608–9. Chapter 7 used with permission of P&R Publishing Co. P.O. Box 817, Phillipsburg, N.J. 08865 www.prpbooks.com

Appendix 7. Special Counsel & Help for Those Closest to Us: Where Do They Fit In?

Historically, more women have had to deal with men (boyfriends, fiancés, and husbands) who have gone off into sensual struggles than vice versa. Not much has been written to help these women respond biblically and with wisdom. Today, however, the number of women struggling with a sensual mind is growing in numbers. Women who don't feel very attractive to men use the Internet, movies, or sensual books as their outlet for their dreams, fantasies, and drives. This means that many Christian men need help to respond biblically with their struggling wives, girlfriends, and fiancées.

For Men and Women Who Are Not Yet Married

If men and women are to recover from pornography and sensuality of heart, their spouses need to be involved in the process. However, this is not a process that the girlfriend, boyfriend, or fiancé(e) should be involved with. Why? Because there is a huge difference between the man or woman you share your bed with and the man or woman you *may* spend your life with. A man's wife, for example, is now part of who he is. She is "one" with the man. His girlfriend, however, is a fellow Christian who shares his goals for life and godliness, but who does not yet own his body or the man himself. The man belongs to Christ both by creation and by regeneration. The girlfriend also belongs to Christ in this way (1 Cor. 6:19–20). Similarly, the man's fiancée is one who has met the preliminary tests of a permanent relationship and whom the man has promised to make a permanent part of his life, but he is not yet ready for that. They are not yet at the point of "no return."

One of the dangers and problems of being a fiancé or fiancée is determining how to handle the "no-man's-land" of emotions and thoughts. However, God is only interested in the black and white of either being married or not. Don't confuse the issue of being *almost married*. You have just discovered your future partner's struggle with his or her thought life. Never before has he or she unburdened to you his or her inner lusts. "So," you ask, "how am I as the fiancé/fiancée to treat this woman/man that I want to marry and have promised to marry?" Simple: put off the wedding. (I know: it is easier said than done; but this is where you have to decide how serious you are about honoring God and preparing for your future vows.) Postpone it. Marriage will not solve the problem. Ask all the men who cheated on their wives or left their families for other women. Ask men who are married and in ministry. Have they struggled with temptation in their thought life? Yes. Ask women who have lived a fantasy life of romantic love based on their romance novels and romantic movies. Have they stopped dreaming and fantasizing about men and the sensual things they will do for them? No. It is true that marriage does temporarily douse the flames of lust, but if you use sex as a part of marriage that is all about you, you do not do justice to God's purpose for the marriage bed. The marriage bed is a place for meeting the desires of your spouse, not for looking to see what you get out of it. And eventually, your self-focused lusts will ignite into either a bonfire or a forest fire that will not be satisfied with the marriage bed.

I remember, early in my ministry, visiting with a dear Christian family. Their eldest son was married and was in his first year or two of bliss. His question to me was, "How do I keep my eyes from wandering?" (He asked me this question in front of his wife, so I knew they had already discussed it together.) He was already struggling with being true to his wife. How could this be? Are men such idiots as to not be satisfied so soon in marriage? Yes, we are. The simple fool of Proverbs is one who needs instruction and help. He is open to change and hope. Most men go into marriage just as untaught as their wives in how this struggle to be faithful and true in thought as well as deed works.

My wife has met with young women who are preparing for marriage. She has asked them what their expectations in marriage are. She has asked them to describe their picture of a wonderful marriage. She has asked them what movies, books, and Internet conversations have been the basis of their "dream marriage" relationship to their men. In one workshop she spent time analyzing the latest movies and books that most of the Christian women of college age were going to see or reading. The not-so-hidden sexual-excitement element was continually in the foreground, luring the reader or the movie watcher in. What will happen when her dream marriage vanishes into thin air? She will go looking for satisfaction on the Internet. Or she will find more books through which her imagination can create its own illicit affairs. These young women have commented to my wife that the lust created by these books and movies leaves them unsatisfied and wanting something more.

Remember: the man who enters marriage with hidden struggles of sensual thinking is satisfying his lust rather than pouring out his love on his wife. The woman who enters marriage with these same hidden struggles is lust-driven to see and fantasize more and imagine what other men would be like if she were in their arms. The man will, if he is honest, use masturbation as his outlet for pleasure and will not find his ultimate satisfaction with his future wife. She will be part of the package of satisfaction, but not the whole deal. Furthermore, she won't know whether he is thinking and fantasizing about her or about his pornographic images when in bed. Likewise, the wife who would be honest with her husband will admit she masturbates or spends time in her fantasy world of novels or movies. She will be looking for the man out in the world around her who will be that romantic, sensual completion of her imagination. Unless God intervenes, an affair and divorce are only a matter of time.

The fiancée is not the one who can be such a man's accountability partner. She should be and will be when and if she becomes his wife. She is currently too emotionally entangled to be objective and careful. She will need counsel and help in keeping her focus on Christ and not wanting to somehow satisfy the man's lust. Her hope tends to be in solving this lust problem by getting her fiancé to the marriage bed. She is blind and foolish in thinking this way, and I say it straight like this because I love you enough to warn you now. The fiancé, too, is not able to think biblically through this struggle. His own hope of being the "man of her dreams" will be crushed. He cannot live up to the fantasy world she has created, any more than can a woman live up the pornographic fantasy world created for a man.

You need to step back from your relationship because this man or woman's thought life is sensual and thus not pure toward you. This is a serious problem. If you enter marriage this way, it will be a disaster. Your boyfriend/girlfriend or fiancé/fiancée needs to have the kind of renewing of the mind and desires that are discussed in this workbook. His or her focus and thinking must be turned toward God and a pursuit of passionate godliness. He or she needs time to demonstrate that 2 Corinthians 7:9–11 has taken place in his or her life (godly sorrow leading to those characteristics). The family, parents, or couple that just rushes into marriage so as to ignore the problem shows a lack of biblical commitment to a godly lifestyle and a pure marriage. Such people show their blindness or, at best, their lack of understanding in this area. They are naive to think that life will all work out OK.

Remember that you can always back out of a dating, courting, or engaged relationship. The Bible has no problem with you doing so. But you should not do that in marriage. If you are thinking about your fiancé, "Well, if he struggles in our marriage and can't kick his pornography habit, I will just ditch him," this is a terrible way to enter marriage. It is like entering into a marriage with other women around. As he walks down the aisle to marry you, he still desires time with Diane, Michel, and Ashley, and later spends online time with them to fulfill his lust (he may not know their names, but he knew their bodies before he knew yours). Equally unfaithful is the woman who enters marriage with Dan, Michael, and Andrew on her mind. She too will struggle to find the marriage satisfactory.

Your final question about your engaged partner will be, "When will we know whether he or she is back on track?" "How will we know that he or she is cured of this problem?" This is difficult. I cannot counsel you outside of your particular situation. Sin is not done in a vacuum. Therefore, the answer will come through the wisdom of your pastor or other biblical counselor who is helping you work through this. Since I have been almost harsh in my negativity regarding continuing down the road toward marriage with this man or woman, I must make it clear that I am not treating him or her as a lost cause. The reality is that if parents or friends tell you to ditch your fiancé/fiancée and move on to someone else, it may be because they believe that he or she is a "pervert" and will never change. I do not say that. They ignore the fact that all men and women have some struggle with their thought lives, and many have fallen into pornography but been rescued by living out the reality of the cross. No label other than "sinner addicted to his or her sin" should be used.

Husbands and Wives

If you are already in this one-flesh relationship, you have a different set of expectations. For one thing, you are committed to a permanent relationship, and God expects you to stay with your man or woman. You must exercise *agapé* love just as Christ did for the church. If you are a wife, you know what it is like to feel like trash and to think yourself less attractive than other women your husband looks at in his lust.

Use the questions below for a time to help give accountability in some major areas and to show up any problems that are hidden. These questions were originally designed for a wife whose husband has fallen and confessed and who is at the start of the path to change, but a husband can adapt them as appropriate to provide accountability for his wife. Don't live your life this way for long.

- Is he doing things with me or avoiding time together?
- Are we going to bed and waking up at the same time?
- Are we staying together at all times when shopping in town?
- Are there any unexplained phone numbers on our account summary?
- Is his cash getting spent inexplicably?
- Is he short with me or easily irritated?
- Is there anything hidden around the house (check briefcase and other things that can be locked)?
- Are we reading and praying together regularly? Is he initiating and leading in this?
- Is his time accounted for when he is home by himself?
- Is he initiating our physical relationship or acting as if he is OK without it?
- Is there a spirit of pride, a lack of dependence on the Lord, or a critical spirit toward others demonstrated on a regular basis?

This is a hard way to live in marriage. The joy and romance are gone and in their place is the river bed of desire gone dry with the drought that sensuality brings. Trust in the relationship has evaporated and has left in its place fear and anger, and perhaps even bitterness, which eats away at the soul. One wife shared with me that she was using the above questions with her husband but felt like the Gestapo in his life. It was necessary because he had gone so far into pornography as to lead a double life. Ultimately, however, he acknowledged the depths of his struggle and sought repentance and help.

Wives, you will need this workbook to help you keep your focus on God and His grace, mercy, and faithfulness. If your focus is on your husband, you will feel like quitting daily. Do not use your children as a crutch or a means to motivate you to stay in the marriage. When they are gone, you will go as well. You have to commit to this broken relationship for the sake of Christ and the gospel. He promises that He will not give you more than you can handle, with the help of His grace. For you, living in the shadow of the cross means that you daily remind yourself of your own sinful drives and thank God for His mercy to you and to your husband.

Husbands, you need to love, date, and woo your wife after marriage just as much as you did before. You need to provide special, loving times together outside of the marriage bed. However, these moments will never meet the unrealistic expectations that have been envisioned in your wife's dream world based on films and literature. That dream world will get shattered by realities that need to be met with gospel hope and joy. A wife who has built up such a fantasy world needs to be brought to the Scriptures to see that it is idolatry and worship of something outside of her marriage. You need to listen to and learn from your wife. You need to be aware of her struggle in her thinking and fantasies. You need lovingly to lead her to the reality and the joy that can be found in marriage. She committed to marrying you and you were not, at any stage of your premarital relationship, the living version of somebody's imagination on the big screen. Thus, her commitment or vow to live with you demands that she destroy the mental and emotional walls of her heart that protect this fornication room. Help her know that you will commit to being the godly husband that God calls you to be.

Appendix 8.
Testimonies of God's Power in Salvation

In this appendix you will find testimonies that show God's grace at work in the lives of two men I have known in ministry and through counsel. I believe their journeys to radical change will encourage you just as they have me.

I am going to start at the very beginning of my story. I hope that this will be an encouragement to many, but I am also praying that the Lord will use this to challenge hearts that need to experience the salvation that only Christ can bring.

> No one who abides in [Christ] keeps on sinning; no one who keeps on sinning has either seen him or known him. Little children, let no one deceive you. Whoever practices righteousness is righteous, as he is righteous. Whoever makes a practice of sinning is of the devil, for the devil has been sinning from the beginning. The reason the Son of God appeared was to destroy the works of the devil. No one born of God makes a practice of sinning, for God's seed abides in him, and he cannot keep on sinning because he has been born of God. By this it is evident who are the children of God, and who are the children of the devil: whoever does not practice righteousness is not of God, nor is the one who does not love his brother. (1 John 3:6–10)

When I was born, my dad was the pastor of a church in lower Michigan. As I grew up, I soon realized what it was like to "be in ministry." Church was a huge part of our lives. Plans were made around church activities and we were always doing something church-related. Church was always a good thing. My whole family enjoyed being at church and loved the people. With dad-for-a-pastor and a pastor-for-a-dad, spiritual things were often discussed in the home.

When I was five years old, our family planned to go to Oklahoma to visit my grandparents. For the first time, we were going to fly. My parents wanted to make sure that I knew that I was saved, since I had never made a profession of salvation. We sat in the living room, they shared the gospel with me, and I told them that I would like to accept Jesus into my heart. I looked back on that day for years as the day that I got saved.

As I grew up, I was an average kid. I knew that my parents expected me to "be a good boy," so I tried to make sure that I was. I never did anything really bad, and generally tried to behave. Looking back now, I can see that many of the "little things" that I struggled with—being kind to others, telling the truth, and so on—were symptoms of a heart condition of which I was completely unaware.

In high school, a good friend of mine introduced me to the biggest struggle of my life. In his basement after school one day before a soccer game, he showed me a pornographic magazine. This first look ignited passions and desires in my flesh that were so strong they controlled my life for the next several years. Throughout the rest of my high-school years I was controlled by and in bondage to my own lusts. James 1:14–15 says, "But each person is tempted when he is lured and enticed by his own desire. Then desire when it has conceived gives birth to sin, and sin when it is fully grown brings forth death." The lust of my heart was the driving force of my life.

These passions and desires only grew stronger, and as I began attending Bible College, things did not improve. I looked for opportunities to indulge my sinful passions and I was unable to control my flesh. I was caught in my sin several times during high school and college, but I always lied and deceived and was able to convince my parents and others around me that I was back on the right track. In my heart, I always knew that I was far from being right with my parents, much less with God. In college I continued to put on a good front before others. I was selected to travel on a promotional team for the school my freshman and sophomore years. We traveled to several churches during the school year and then went for several weeks during the summer. I really enjoyed the ministry opportunity that God had given me. After all, a pastor's kid should be "in the ministry," right?

I met my wife during my freshman year. She played the piano for our traveling group. Eventually, we began to get interested in each other. Between my junior and senior years, we were married at her home church in Murfreesboro, Tennessee. Yet still in my heart, sin thrived. Marriage did not take away the desire to fulfill the lusts of the flesh. I took every opportunity that I could find to satisfy my sinful desires. The Internet as well as TV/DVD pornography began to fill my need for filth. As with all sin, I began to crave more and more. I needed new highs and new levels of excitement. I began to use the phone to try to get satisfaction. This led me to depths of sin that I never thought that I would reach.

While at college my wife and I lived in a small eight-family apartment building. I was going to finish my schooling and then we were going to head out west to work in a church and eventually plant a church—all of this was planned while sin was ruling my life. At college, I began to find ways to use other people's phones to fulfill my lust. I figured that I would not get caught. However, one day a police car arrived on campus and my boss, the head of security, called me into a meeting. Some of the administration were present, as well as the police officer. They questioned me as to my involvement with the phone abuse. I denied any involvement, but finally buckled when threatened with a polygraph test—a lie detector. This incident led to my dismissal about three weeks before I was due to graduate. We moved to Michigan, and attended my home church, where my dad still pastors, for eight to nine months. I was hoping to return to finish my schooling the next year.

In October, I received a letter from a lawyer in Wisconsin, who wanted to represent me when I went to court. This was a shock to me, since the police told me that they were not pressing charges. Those I had wronged at the college also expressed a spirit of forgiveness toward me. I called to find out what I was being charged with and then began to try to find out what I needed to do next. I found a Christian lawyer who took my case and we headed off to court in mid-January. I was anticipating a fine but not jail, since the D.A. was not asking for any time. However, the judge decided that I was to serve ninety days. I went to the County Jail and spent the loneliest three months of my life. I got many encouraging letters from my wife, my family, and many friends—almost all of them encouraging me to stay strong in the Lord. However, I still was not able to get victory over my lust. Although (surprisingly) pornography was not allowed in the jail, I was every bit as much addicted to it when I was released as I was when I went in.

Life continued. I got a job at a sawmill and I finished college—I graduated with a degree in Pastoral Studies. Still, sin gripped me. I was always trying to sneak a look here and there ... trying to satisfy my desires. Several times my wife caught me in moral failure and I would always "repent" and try to do better. Early in February one year, my wife discovered more filth and called our pastor. He came to our house and met with me. After a long discussion, I told him that I did not know how to get lasting victory over my sin. He began to take me to the Scriptures and explain to me, again, how to live the victorious Christian life. I told him that it did not work for me. I explained that I had tried all the things that different people had recommended, only to end up frustrated and no less in bondage than before. At that, he began to take me to passages that describe the life of the believer—1 John; 1 Corinthians 2:10–3:3; Romans 8:1–17; Hebrews 4:12; 12:1–11. He challenged me to really pray through these passages, and said that we needed to meet again the next week. About three weeks passed and because of sickness and other circumstances, we did not meet. Finally, he called me one Saturday to ask if he could stop by and talk. I told him that I had done nothing concerning the passages that he had left with me, and said that I would call him when I was ready to talk to him. I did not go to church the next morning. Monday came and I went to work. I was glad to go since things had been pretty awkward in our home over the weekend.

My job as a worker with saws requires me to be in a cab all day long by myself. As I was working that day, I began to think of the verses that our pastor had shared with me. Since I was sure that I had been saved, I started trying to convince God that I was saved. I continued to offer excuses in my mind as the Holy Spirit would bring verse after verse to my remembrance. Finally, I came to the place where God's Word convinced me that my experience was not aligned with the Scripture's description of the believer's life. I knew that according to the Word of God, I was not a believer. This was a hard realization for me. After all, I grew up a pastor's kid, went to Christian school, ... I stood there sawing and realized that either I was right or God's Word was right. When I came home that night, I told my wife of the struggle that had been going on in my heart and asked her if she would like to pray with me, because I knew that I needed Christ. I knew that I did not have a real relationship with God. I knew that I was of my father—the devil. We went into our bedroom and she prayed first. I then told the Lord that I knew that I had trusted in myself and the words that I said that day when I was five for my salvation. I asked Him to become my Savior. James 1:18 sums up my experience so well! It says, "Of his own will he brought us forth by the word of truth, that we should be a kind of firstfruits of his creatures."

This is just the beginning of a new life for me. I am so thankful that God is a longsuffering God. It has been encouraging to experience the real joy of knowing Christ and His power in my life. For the first time there is a hunger for the Word and a joy in Christ! I know that Satan has not given up on me and that my struggle with sin is far from over, but I am so thankful for God's indwelling Spirit and the power to overcome sin.

Second Corinthians 5:17 says, "Therefore, if anyone is in Christ, he is a new creation. The old has passed away; behold, the new has come."

As I sit down to write this I have many mixed emotions that flood into my mind as I think back over the past year. God has certainly taken me on quite a journey! Most of this story is my personal one, as most of what has been going on involves me specifically. But, since I now have a family, it has impacted and affected them as well. Although we are currently in a place of much joy and excitement about what God has for us in the future, most of what I am going to share involves a lot of hurt, sorrow, heartache, and sin. It's hard for me to recount all of this and work through all the feelings that come with it, but it is necessary for telling my story and so that you can understand.

Before we go further, I want to say that all of the glory *must* go to God! While some of this story came as a shock to those who knew me, I want you to know the depths of what happened in my life so that we can all rejoice together in the work of Christ. This then, is my story.

I grew up as the eldest of six children, and my parents were part of a ministry which involved spending ten months out of every year on the road traveling across the country and ministering in thousands of churches. Through high school I worked in the children's clubs, teaching stories, leading songs, and sharing Christ with them. After high school, I raised support and traveled as a singer on the team for two years. After that, I headed off to Bible college, where I studied music and the Bible, participated in numerous student activities, and was a part of a traveling singing/drama team each year. Between my junior and senior years, I interned at a church in Holland, Michigan, as a music "pastor" and led in worship, preached a couple times, and helped out in the ministry there. After graduating from college, I married my one and only girlfriend and we started out on this journey of life. We moved to Holland, Michigan, where I took a job teaching at a small Christian school connected to our home church. I taught music classes (K–12th grade), led the many choirs, taught Bible classes, directed several musicals, pretty much oversaw the whole Fine Arts Program, and even did some janitorial work the first year and a half! During those four and a half years, my wife gave birth to our daughters (in 2004 and 2007). I write all of this because at this point in my life, when I look back at all the ministry that I was doing and involved in, I am struck with awe that through all of that I could still have missed something. From what God has revealed to me in recent months, I was able to go through all of that and still not "get" it!

The bottom line is that, for years, I have struggled (sometimes off and on) with sexual sin. I became involved in Internet pornography, to the point that I could easily deceive myself into thinking that it was just something I would "struggle" with and which would remain private: something to deal with on the side. After all, look at all that "I" was able to accomplish in ministry. I can't say that my sin was such a driving force in my younger years, but the visual struggle was there at times, lingering in the back of my brain. But after I got married, and especially during my wife's first pregnancy, when she was extremely sick, those temptations began to creep back in and take control. And I yielded to them. It was this particular area of sin that eventually cost me my teaching job and was the real reason why I had to resign in January 2007. My sin had been discovered and although I was "repentant" at the time, everyone felt that it was the best option for me and my family. I had hurt them and needed to step out of the ministry spotlight (which I craved) and focus on what was most important: my walk with Christ and my family.

The true reason for my resigning wasn't shared with anyone publicly, since my sin did not directly involve anyone but me. In fact, only the few people that we felt closest to knew, because we would share with them in hopes of accountability and help through the process. For several months, things seemed to get better. My wife and I were communicating better, and although the job I had now taken (working for Panera Bread) caused finances to become very tight, we seemed to be working through things and starting to sort life out. But the truth was that I was still holding on to sin and trying to "fight" it on my own without my wife knowing what was going on. I had deceived myself into thinking that it would all eventually pass when, in actuality, I was in bondage and needed help. We attended a "Basics of Marriage" counseling class together, along with some friends, in order to focus on our relationship and work through some healing and other issues that we both wanted to grow in. That time proved to be amazing and very exciting for us, as we really felt God working and changing some things. Still, through all of this, I didn't tell my wife about my struggles and how I was still battling the fleshly desires that waged inside me.

All this continued until one day in late November 2008, when a good friend asked if he could come over and talk with us. Little did I know that he was coming over to confront me about my sin and some things that he had observed. So there, in front of my poor wife, who had no idea that I was still struggling and yielding to the lusts of my eyes, he confronted me over my sin. I just sat and tried to deny and justify and defend. My wife was in shock and even tried to defend me until she realized that I had not been honest with her about my struggle. After a very long period of my sitting still, stubbornly resisting the Holy Spirit as He tried to break through in my heart, my friend finally asked a question that got to the heart of the issue: "When would you say was the high point in your walk with Christ? When would you say you were closest to Him and walking in obedience and close fellowship with Him?"

It was something I had asked myself before and sometimes struggled with, but I had never wanted to spend much time on it or even go there. After all, look at "all that I had done" and all that I had been involved with throughout my life. But I honestly couldn't come up with an answer, so I made something up about that time being when I was in college, or something lame like that. "That seems like a long time ago ...," he replied in a thoughtful way. And then it came: I knew what the problem was and fear rushed into my heart, instantly followed by a million reasons and arguments as to why it couldn't be true. But I knew that the issue was a matter of my heart. I finally broke down and confessed to my friend and to my wife that it was all true. I sat and sobbed like a baby and just couldn't stop. I felt completely ashamed, alone, and so grieved over my sin. I named my sins by name. My friend left, telling us that he would be praying for us.

I had been sitting on the floor during the whole ordeal and had been so tense that my back was starting to hurt badly. I had to lie down. Amazingly enough, our girls were quiet and playing in their room, which gave my wife and me time to talk. I told her that I knew what I needed to do, but I was scared. To think that twenty-nine years of my life had passed without me truly knowing Christ as my Savior! But when I looked back at years of ministry life and "serving" God, I realized that it was all motivated by my exterior surroundings and a desire to receive the applause of men! It wasn't done out of a heart that truly followed Christ and had a vibrant relationship with Him. In fact, when all those external things were stripped away from me, the place I would run for "comfort" and "fulfillment" was my sin! So I told my wife what I needed ... I needed Christ! We went to our bedroom and I cried out to God and asked Him to forgive me for my sins and to truly save me and become Lord and Master of my life. Our eldest daughter came into the room and saw me crying and praying. She began crying too, and I told God, "Before my wife and my precious daughter here, I ask You to save me and change me and take control of my life!" What a powerful moment that was for me! I will never forget that evening! After I prayed, I was able to explain to our daughter what Daddy was crying about and what had just happened!

Later that night, I pulled out a new journal that my dad had given me just a few weeks earlier and wrote in the front of it, "My Spiritual Journey Finally Begins, November 19, 2008. praise the lord!" Since that day, I have experienced such joy and freedom every time I have been able to share my story with friends and family. That, of course, was the hardest and scariest moment for me ... when I had the opportunity to share my testimony with our family. Yet I was completely overwhelmed by the love and support that they offered and the sweet fellowship that came when I was able to openly share all that God had been doing over the previous year. The following Christmas was absolutely *amazing*—a wonderful time of renewal and rejoicing in the precious gift of God's Son! It was my first Christmas as a true child of God!

I have learned so much from all of this. I know now that following Christ is a daily, moment-by-moment, conscious decision for those of us who claim His salvation. I am learning that I need to be "ravenous for the Word" and desire to read, meditate on, and apply it to *every* area of my life! God has directed me in several steps of obedience to put up safeguards for my life as I begin this genuine walk with Him. I continue to work on surrendering the things of this world that I once loved and to give everything up for Him. I am so thankful right now for my wonderful and forgiving wife, who has gone with me on this journey and has been so supportive and encouraging. God has grown our relationship by leaps and bounds through all of this. We are extremely thankful for the church we are currently a part of and active in. They have been incredibly supportive and encouraging to us through this whole process. We are excited to grow closer together and closer to Christ.

Although ministry has always been such a huge part of my life and something that I used to try to find security and confidence in, I can truly say now, for the first time ever, that if the only ministry I have in life from this point forward is the ministry to my wife and children, that is enough: that is all I need for fulfillment. They are my ministry and the most important people in my life. We have no idea what God has for our future, but for now, we are simply rejoicing in God's work of salvation and extremely thankful for the power of the cross and for finally breaking through my stubborn heart. I have to remind myself over and over that God's timing is always perfect. And although this is not the way either of us ever pictured our lives, we are so glad that God has finally stripped away all the exterior walls around my life and shown me my true self. I am so thankful for the love, forgiveness, and the blood of Jesus Christ. I have many regrets from my past, but God continually shows me the need to press forward and live day by day now and be the light of Christ to everyone around me.

Thank you for taking the time to read this lengthy story. I hope that it has been an encouragement to you and a testimony of God's goodness! We truly serve an awesome and Almighty God!

Appendix 9. Purity Survey

If you are counseling, discipling, or meeting with others in small groups, this survey can help you gain an understanding of the personal journey of those you are helping and of their specific battles. You may also find that by working through the survey with others, it will provide common ground for the help to be found within the Christian community.

Help on Purity
1. Did anyone ever discuss your body and its development with you? Yes / No
❑ Parent ❑ Pastor/Youth pastor ❑ Friend ❑ Sibling/relative
2. Did you have help in setting up personal purity standards as a teen? Yes / No
From ❑ Parent ❑ Pastor/Youth pastor ❑ Friend ❑ Sibling/relative
3. Did these standards involve use of the Internet?
4. Did these standards involve TV or movie watching?
5. Did you have help in finding Bible principles for purity? Yes / No
6. Did your parents set dating guidelines for you? Yes / No
7. Did you date or have some kind of serious relational involvement with someone of the opposite sex as a teenager? Yes / No
8. Did you allow physical contact in this relationship? Yes / No
9. Did you get more involved physically than you planned? Yes / No

Internet
1. Have you had access to the Internet? Yes / No
Where? ❑ At home ❑ At school ❑ Other places
2. Was there a filter or accountability in this setting? Yes / No
3. Have you ever accessed material on the Internet that was immoral? Yes / No
❑ Accidentally stumbled across it. Did you go back and find more?
❑ Intentionally found some.
4. Which area of the Internet is the most tempting for you?
❑ Sports sites ❑ Social networking ❑ Gaming ❑ Movie sites ❑ Other

Personal Morality Struggles
1. Have you struggled with pornography in any form at any time? Yes / No
If yes, did you get help in overcoming this struggle? Yes / No
From whom: ❑ Parent ❑ Pastor/Youth pastor ❑ Friend ❑ Sibling/relative
Would you like some help/further help in this area? Yes / No
2. Have you ever struggled with masturbation? Yes / No
  • Did you have help in overcoming this problem? Yes / No
  • Would you like some help/further help? Yes / No
  • Has anyone ever discussed masturbation to you using Scripture? Yes / No

- Do you understand the difference between masturbation and "wet dreams"?
  Yes / No

3. Do you believe that the accountability you have is enough to help you be victorious in purity areas? Yes / No

If not, would you come and talk about this with us? Yes / No

4. What was or has been the length of your struggle?
   ❑ Short
   ❑ Some months
   ❑ 1–2 years
   ❑ Off and on over several years

5. What would you call "success" in this area?

Appendix 10. Renew the Mind

As part of the process of renewing the mind and building new patterns, it helps to make a comparison between what I *was* ("putting off the old man") and what I *want to be in Christ* ("putting on the new man"). In the chart below, the "Pride" versus "Humility" columns explore the ways in which pride will control us and keep us from humbly seeking help and desiring to change. The "Desires for more" come out of hearts that are not thankful toward God. We must see what a thankful heart looks, thinks, and acts like. Finally, finding pleasure in self must be contrasted with finding pleasure in God. The more we see the ways in which we live to please self, and the more we hate it, the more satisfaction and pleasure in living for God we will find. This new kind of life (pleasing God) is radically different from a life of pleasing self.

Pride v. Humility
Desire for more v. Thankfulness
Self-pleasure v. God Pleasure

Pride	Humility
I can handle this	I need God's Spirit & grace
I am doing well	I could fall anytime without God
I went 6 months without falling	I have been free from sensuality by God's grace
I won't let this control me	I want God's control
I am different from porn addicts	I could be addicted to sin as well
I would never let sensuality go that far	I won't see how far sin takes me
I can give up my sin when I want to	I can't put sin away on my own without God
I can't admit to the church what I do	I need to embrace the church's loving disciple-ship
I am driven by the fear of man and a love of myself	I am driven by the fear of God and a heart of love for Him
I have lived for God and done a lot of good work for His church	God has helped me please Him and I am humbled to serve His church
Desire for More	Thankful for God
I need a better wife	God is all I need
I want things this world enjoys too	His gifts are wonderful beyond description
I want more self-pleasure	My greatest pleasure is in God not self
I prefer many friends but not too tight	God is my most intimate friend
My goal is to be the best	I will go as far as God takes me

I deserve a break from pressure	I deserve hell, but have been given God
I should get the approval of others	I am accepted in Christ by the Father
I have been treated poorly	I will never be treated by God as a sinner
Self Pleasure	God Pleasure
Dominated by self	Dominated by God
Satisfying the lust of the flesh	Finding satisfaction in Him alone
Longing to see the forbidden of this world; tantalized by what I shouldn't have	Longing to enjoy His grace and goodness; longing for what I can't see in the next world
Wanting to be free from controls	Wanting to be free from the power of sin
Opening the doors of my heart to the lusts of the flesh	Opening my heart to the wonders and glories of God in all His awesome beauty
Captive to and controlled by my flesh and its desires	Captive to Christ, the gospel, and His cross
Serve self and its wretched longings which are never quite satisfied	Serve the One who has already given me the Water of Life that never runs dry
Blown away by the senses of the flesh	Overwhelmed by the God of Glory in my spirit
Pornography pleasure	Pure pleasure and joys of God

Resources

Alcorn, Randy, *The Purity Principle* (Colorado Springs: Multnomah, 2003). Includes practical guidelines for singles, married couples, and parents who wish to train their children in purity. This short book challenges us to take the high road in remaining pure and to reap the benefits that come from it. Some mature content.

Arterburn, Stephen, Stoeker, Fred, and **Yorkey, Mike,** *Every Man's Battle: Winning the War on Sexual Temptation One Victory at a Time* (Colorado Springs: Waterbrook Press, 2000). A strong text for mature men. If you struggle with sensual images, you may want to move quickly through or avoid entirely the story lines included.

Bridges, Jerry, *I Exalt You, O God* (Colorado Springs: Waterbrook Press, 2001). A great help in worship of God. Use it daily.

——*Joy of Fearing God* (Colorado Springs: Waterbrook Press, 1999). An exposition of this theme as it applies to life.

Harris, Josh, *Sex Is Not the Problem, Lust Is* (Colorado Springs: Multnomah, 2003). Excellent material. He has a great chapter on a biblical view of masturbation. Previously titled *Not Even a Hint*, this book is great reading for any man, married or single.

Hughes, R. Kent, *Disciplines of a Godly Man* (Wheaton, IL: Crossway, 1991). Good, practical sections.

Hummel, Rand, *Lest You Fall* (Greenville, SC: JourneyForth, 2005). This short book is excellent for getting started with biblical meditation. A needed help in today's church.

Janz, Jason, *Alone With God* (Greenville, SC: JourneyForth, 2006). An excellent help in building a walk with God. His material on meditation is helpful for a pure life focus on God.

Lambert, Heath, *Finally Free: Fighting for Purity with the Power of Grace* (Grand Rapids: Zondervan, 2013). Heath has written a readable and practical help that is based on solid theology.

Lundgaard, Kris, *The Enemy Within: Straight Talk about the Power and Defeat of Sin* (Phillipsburg, NJ: P&R, 1998). Drawing from *Indwelling Sin* and *The Mortification of Sin* by Puritan John Owen, Lundgaard aims for the heart with a battle plan for radical spiritual transformation.

Piper, John, and **Taylor, Justin,** (eds.), *Sex and the Supremacy of Christ* (Wheaton, IL: Crossway, 2005).

Tozer, A. W., *The Knowledge of the Holy* (New York: HarperCollins, 1978). A great primer on the attributes of God and a basis for meditation on His character.

Booklets

New Growth Press produces titles on behalf of the Christian Counseling and Educational Foundation (CCEF). Many are very relevant, such as:

Clark, Jayne V., *Single and Lonely: Finding the Intimacy You Desire*

Lane, Timothy, *Sex Before Marriage: How Far is Too Far?*

Powlison, David, *Renewing Intimacy: Closing the Gap Between You and Your Spouse*

Smith, Winston T., *Help! My Spouse Committed Adultery: First Steps for Dealing with Betrayal*
——*It's All About Me: The Problem with Masturbation*

Croft, Brian, *Help! He's Struggling With Pornography* (Leominster: Day One, 2010). The blurb says, "How can a Christian man find victory over pornography? This booklet presents the only true solution: God's power working through the gospel within the context of the local church."

Related Topics

SEX

Schaumburg, Harry, *Undefiled: Redemption from Sexual Sin, Restoration for Broken Relationships* (Chicago: Moody, 2010). Schaumburg writes about finding redemption from sexual sin and seeks to help couples find restoration for breaking or broken relationships. Monergism Books has bundled a whole lot of resources into one "Sexual Redemption Bundle" based around Harry Schaumburg's *Undefiled*—visit www.monergismbooks.com.

——*False Intimacy: Understanding the Struggle of Sexual Addiction* (Colorado Springs, CO: NavPress, 1997). This book includes the struggle with homosexuality and cybersex.

Wheat, Ed., M.D., and **Gaye,** *Intended for Pleasure: Sex Technique and Sexual Fulfillment in Christian Marriage* (Grand Rapids, MI: Revell, 2010). This is a nuts-and bolts kind of book that is often given to newlyweds to help them get "oriented" in the bedroom. Many couples who aren't given one before they get married end up trying to track one down during their honeymoon.

WOMEN

Mahaney, Carolyn, *Feminine Appeal* (Wheaton, IL: Crossway, 2003). A book for women in which Mahaney challenges them on a host of issues related to love, sex, and marriage.

Jaynes, Sharon, *Becoming the Woman of His Dreams* (Eugene, OR: Harvest House, 2005). I haven't done more than skim this one, but it comes highly recommended by others. I found Jaynes particularly strong in her description of how men perceive sex and its importance to them.

DeMoss, Nancy Lee, *Lies Women Believe* (Chicago: Moody, 2002). Helps uncover how everyone, including men, is subtly deceived by today's society. DeMoss inspects popular beliefs held by most Western women and clearly shows how they deviate from the simple, undeniable truth as written in God's Word. Great for small groups.

Thorne, Hellen, *Purity Is Possible: How to Live Free of the Fantasy Trap* (Epsom, Surrey, England: The Good Book Company, 2014). Hellen describes her own struggles with lust and shares how she has gained increased victory over the sin. She writes in a friendly and conversational tone.

Web Sites

www.ccef.org/ The Christian Counseling and Educational Foundation offers counseling and excellent resources on a number of issues (including the New Growth Press titles mentioned above).

www.boundless.org/ Boundless Webzine, targeted at Christian singles and young adults. A great resource.

www.stonegateresources.org/ Stone Gate Resources offers brief intensive counseling for couples who are in need of immediate help. If your marriage is on the rocks due to sex-related issues, this is a good place to seek help.

www.challies.com/topics/pornography. As an online blogger, few people have access to more resources and information like Tim Challies.

About the Author

D r. Dave Coats is a pastor, counselor, and teacher who enjoys the privilege of serving God. He has been on a journey of faith and ministry that has taken him from the western mountains and desert of the United States, to the beautiful backwoods of the north Midwest, to the Caribbean of Haiti, and to the eastern coast of Canada.

Dave's passion is learning of and living out the reality of the death of Christ and the power of His resurrection in his own life as well as helping others to know the same. His journey has been greatly enhanced and made more fun by having his wife Judi at his side through all the adventures and challenges of living for God. They enjoy sharing in the fellowship of the gospel with their grown children and young grandchildren that God has given them.

Dave is a certified biblical counselor with ACBC and loves to see how God uses the Word to address people's problems. He has also taught biblical counseling in three different countries and has lead a counseling program at the university level. One of his desires is to help people to put aside the secular means of dealing with the troubles that they experience in this world and to help them to see that God has a superior understanding and power to help people change and to become what God designed them to be.

Dave and Judi wrote the Life-Line mini-book Help! My Teen Is Rebellious. They are also presently working on a book about the proverbs of Solomon. Judi does editing and writing for publications and serves as a resource for teaching grammar, having taught English at university level for almost two decades. Dave pastors, teaches, and does work in their rural, northern Wisconsin area. Dave and Judi run Longview Farm Vacation Rental, a place where people come to enjoy the beauty and fun of the northwoods of Wisconsin.

You may connect with Dave at www.coatscounsel.net.

or on Facebook at https://www.facebook.com/david.a.coats.9